More prai

"In this time of cataclysm and convulsion, Dan issues a clarion call to make the inward journey to the land of the Spirit to do the inner work that will fully activate our human agency to fashion a compassionate and just society. This gem of a book is a training manual for those of us who are serious about heeding the prophet Micah's call to do justice, love mercy, and walk humbly with God."
—Rev. Gregory Bentley, Co-Moderator of the 224th General Assembly of the PC(USA)

"*Looking Inward, Living Outward* is a transformative book that delves deep into the intersection of contemplative spirituality and social transformation. With practical wisdom, Wolpert navigates us through a series of contemplative practices designed to integrate our sense of inner calling and outward action. By addressing fundamental questions about deepening spiritual practices, the book offers a holistic approach to spiritual growth and societal change. Highly recommend it!"
—Rev. Cameron Trimble, CEO of Convergence, Partner at FutureWomenX, and author of *Searching for the Sacred*

"Like his spiritual guide, Jesus of Nazareth preaching his sermon on the mount, Wolpert teaches us how to participate with God's transforming work in the world. To do so requires both contemplative retreat and loving action. As the physical body must breathe in and out to stay alive; our spirits must look inward and live outward. Wolpert describes this sacred rhythm that keeps our spirits breathing with vitality as we serve God's kin-dom . . . on earth as it is in heaven."
—Frank Rogers Jr., Muriel Bernice Roberts Professor of Spiritual Formation and Narrative Pedagogy and Co-Director of the Center for Engaged Compassion, Claremont Theological Seminary; author of *Practicing Compassion and Cradled in the Arms of Compassion: A Spiritual Journey from Trauma to Recovery*

"With wisdom and clarity, Wolpert invites us to embrace a life grounded in spiritual practice, oriented to the here-and-now, expressed in peace-loving, justice-seeking, compassionate action in the world. In a world heavy with suffering, stress, and spiritual dis-ease, this is the book we need, challenging us to grasp the "upside-down kingdom teachings of the Gospel" and to embody them faithfully. Read this book and be inspired to look inward and live outward: two dimensions of an integrated spiritual life in pursuit of beloved community."
—**Rev. Dr. Allen Ewing-Merrill, Executive Director, The BTS Center**

"These are crushing times. We are witnessing the violent edges of empire in every sphere. Our hearts are left broken. Bayo Akomolafe says, 'Times are urgent, slow down.' This is a book that takes this contradiction seriously. Let us tend to our souls. Listen for the spirit. And fight with everything we've got for a world more beautiful than we can hope to imagine."
—**Lydia Wylie-Kellermann, author of** *This Sweet Earth: Walking with our Children in the Age of Climate Collapse*

LOOKING INWARD, LIVING OUTWARD

LOOKING INWARD, LIVING OUTWARD

THE SPIRITUAL PRACTICE OF SOCIAL TRANSFORMATION

DANIEL WOLPERT

LOOKING INWARD, LIVING OUTWARD: The Spiritual Practice of Social Transformation
Copyright © 2024 by Daniel Wolpert
All rights reserved.

No part of this book may be reproduced in any manner whatsoever without permission except for brief quotations in critical articles or reviews. For information, write Upper Room Books®, 1908 Grand Avenue, Nashville, TN 37212.

Upper Room Books® website: upperroombooks.com

Upper Room®, Upper Room Books®, and design logos are trademarks owned by The Upper Room®, Nashville, Tennessee. All rights reserved.

Scripture quotations not otherwise marked are from the New Revised Standard Version, Updated Edition. Copyright © 2021 National Council of Churches of Christ in the United States of America. Used by permission. All rights reserved worldwide.

Scripture quotations marked RSV are from the Revised Standard Version of the Bible, copyright © 1946, 1952, and 1971 the Division of Christian Education of the National Council of the Churches of Christ in the United States of America. Used by permission. All rights reserved.

At the time of publication, all websites referenced in this book were valid. However, due to the fluid nature of the internet, some addresses may have changed or the content may no longer be relevant.

Cover design: Molly von Borstel, Faceout Studio
Imagery: Shutterstock
Interior design and typesetting: PerfecType | Nashville, TN

ISBN: 978-0-8358-2051-6
Epub ISBN: 978-0-8358-2052-3

For Humanity: a deep prayer and hope
for our collective evolution

TABLE OF CONTENTS

	Introduction	11
1	Creating Focus in My Life *The Practice of Willful Attention*	21
2	Where Do I Put My Effort? *The Practice of Boundary Creation*	33
3	Who Is Blessed? *The Practice of Fearless Humility*	45
4	Using Our Good Eye *The Practice of Self-Awareness*	59
5	On Becoming Salt and Light *The Practice of Powerful Presence*	73
6	On Oaths and Caring *The Practice of Compassionate Relationship*	87
7	Let's Talk about Money *The Practice of Serving God*	99
8	Facing Anxiety *The Practice of Radical Trust*	109

TABLE OF CONTENTS

9	On Clinging to Treasures *The Practice of Letting Go*	119
10	What Is Justice? *The Practice of Discernment*	129
11	Creating Peace *The Practice of Loving Your Enemy*	143
12	Social Transformation and the Coming Kingdom *The Practice of Prayer*	155
Notes		171

INTRODUCTION

When I began taking the spiritual life seriously, now over four decades ago, it never occurred to me that this life of prayer was somehow separate from social transformation. Perhaps this was because I'd already been involved in activist circles before coming to contemplation. Perhaps it was just my intuition. Whatever the reason, it always seemed obvious to me that we engage our spiritual lives to make the world a better place—to make society more just, more peaceful, more loving. Yet, all these years later, I still encounter people who see a divide between "action" and "contemplation." Thus, I am convinced of the need for this book.

The reasons for this divide lie in the history of the church, particularly since the Reformation, and in the history of our society, particularly since the Industrial Revolution. Doing and activity are what our world values. Action, goals, objectives, and effectiveness are the coin of the realm. And so, spirituality, contemplation, meditation, appear to be the opposite of these things. These activities are viewed as personal, a turning inward away from society. But really, they are just two sides of the same coin.

Luckily, people are becoming more aware of this intimate connection between our inner and outer life. Those who work in activist spaces are realizing they need time apart to reflect, connect deeply with the source of their power, and spend time discerning wise actions. Similarly, those who begin with contemplation increasingly recognize the need to manifest the fruits of the Spirit in a communal life that gives life to all. We are understanding that social transformation is a spiritual practice.

The purpose of this work is to describe and explore a series of practices that promote and support the work of social transformation as we intentionally live in harmony with the Spirit at work in the world. The book will provide some answers to the following questions: How do we move toward what Jesus called the kingdom of God?[1] How do we live a life with God?

What Is Social Transformation?

First, I need to share a few of my basic assumptions and perspectives as I approach this work. These issues will be explored in greater depth in the chapters that follow, but they are important to clarify from the start.

Society is changing all the time. In this sense, transformation is always happening. We are moving from one form to another, and we are doing so fast. We have experienced more change during our lifetimes than any other group of people in the history of the world. It's hard to believe that in high school, I was using a slide rule (Google it!) in science class, and now I carry around a veritable supercomputer in my pocket.

So, from one point of view, we do not need to do anything to cause or create social transformation because it is simply a part of life. But the type of transformation that arises naturally out of human activity and effort is what we might call *unconscious transformation*. Using a term from non-Christian sources, it is the transformation brought about by karmic flow, the flow and action of habitual pattern. We can see this when there is an article about a new technology and people are saying, "Maybe we should pause and think about what we are doing before we go any further with this (new thing)." Yet such reflection is quickly ignored as we plow ahead with the latest gizmos. The pull and movement of our life in the world is irresistible.

The teachings of the spiritual life understand that people always do things that bring change, yet we do most of this activity unconsciously and from the perspective of our ego-self. In fact, such transformation is often exactly the opposite of what God wants. We can see this drama of ego-driven change in the many biblical stories that show God pleading with the people NOT to do something, yet the pleas fall on deaf ears. One of the best examples of this behavior is found in 1 Samuel 8 where God tells the people they shouldn't have a king because a king will oppress them, but they ignore God's advice and insist on having a king just like the other nations that surround them. This habit-driven transformation is not what we are exploring in this book.

Rather, the transformation sought by the spiritual life is in sync with the activity of the Spirit. It is change that intentionally moves in harmony with the creation of the beloved community. Spiritual transformation wants to move from the form of the subconscious, habitual world to the form of a world infused with awareness, justice, and love. This book is about conscious transformation.

On Guilt and Shame

I've been teaching spiritual practice long enough to know many of the pitfalls and sticking points of doing this work in Christian circles. Feelings of guilt and shame are two of the most significant of these problems, which is why I feel the need to address them before beginning to introduce the practices. Sadly, many Christian communities specialize in instilling guilt and shame. We are told we are bad, we are sinners, we are selfish. This message, much like the message that God is an old White guy up on a throne, creeps into even the most forgiving, inviting, and self-aware communities. Feelings of guilt and shame result from an individualistic Christian theology that sees our spiritual life from the binary perspective of *saved* or *not-saved*. Either we are bad, not saved, and doing the wrong things or we are saved, having done the one magical right thing to get saved. While such an understanding might be seen as a very simplistic Christianity, it is none the less a very common theological framework. Viewed through this lens, new spiritual teachings inspire guilt and shame because any new teaching triggers the idea that our previous spiritual activity was somehow wrong.

I have seen repeatedly how some Christians hear new teachings on spirituality as a judgment. The message they receive is, "I'm not doing spirituality right, and I feel bad and need to work harder to do it better." Of course, we cannot stop our feelings from appearing. I would never say, "Don't feel this way"; however, we can choose how we work with our feelings as they arise.

I encourage all who engage in spiritual practice to view it as a journey of self-compassion and curiosity, rather than of guilt or shame. The point of this book isn't to make you feel bad about what you are *not* doing, but rather to invite you into more profound ways of engaging a life with God. Our spiritual life isn't about finding the one right answer. It is a journey of going deeper. Whatever has led you to this book has been part of your path, and now you are entering the next stage of your journey.

When I used to work construction, each morning I would get my tools together and head out to work. Sometimes I would realize that I could use a new tool for my job, and I'd go buy it. I didn't feel guilt or shame because I didn't already have the tool and learning about a new tool did not call into question all the work I had done in the past. I was happy that I'd learned about this new way of working, and I looked forward to the positive results that my new tool would bring.

This is how I'd encourage you to approach spiritual teachings: You are receiving new tools, and you can be excited about the beautiful growth your relationship with God will experience through their use.

Here and Now Orientation and Traveling Companion

The issue of guilt and shame in connection with Christianity is closely connected to the issue of heaven and hell and the focus on the afterlife in of much of Christian teaching. I'll have more to say about this in chapter 1, but I want to be explicit right up front: My reading of Jesus' teachings is that they are not about what happens after death; they are how God is calling us to live while we are here on earth.

This fits with the idea of our spiritual life as a journey through our material existence. We are always growing, always changing, always facing the opportunity to wake up to discern God's call. The problem of humanity is here on this planet. It is the problem of war and violence, greed, poverty, and oppression. These are the problems the spiritual life seeks to address. This doesn't mean that eternal life isn't also a part of the good news; it is, but the spiritual masters of our faith all encourage us to begin the walk toward eternal life here and now. This is the true focus of the practice of social transformation.

In my other books on "life with God," I used traveling companions to help illustrate the practices I was discussing in each chapter.[2] I've found this to be a helpful approach to understanding spiritual practices, and it's also congruent with the practice of having teachers who help us along the way. In this work, I also have a traveling companion, but instead of using multiple people, I am going to use one person and one set of teachings: Jesus and the Sermon on the Mount (see Matthew, chapters 5-7).

Each practice will be grounded in one part of the sermon. I am not going to use every part of his talk, nor will I go in order through the three chapters. Obviously, this is a particular choice of mine, and others could use the material differently. I believe that my approach is consistent with the tone and tenor of all the teachings of this most famous sermon.

Outline of Chapters

In this work, I describe twelve practices that are available to individuals and communities who are interested in social transformation. I've divided these loosely into four parts, each containing three practices. As I describe these methods for engaging the Spirit, both here and later in the book, I want to remind you that spiritual practices are simple but not easy. I suspect that some people will read this summary and think, *Wow, those are no big deal, I've heard of all this before.* There is some truth to this; they sound very simple. Jesus' sermon sounds very simple. But if these practices were easy, our world would be a much different place. So let us stay open to the great depth that these deceptively and paradoxically simple practices can bring to our existence as we allow God to enter our collective lives and transform us.

The first three chapters contain practices that lay the groundwork for engaging in social transformation. These practices create the environment to listen for God and align ourselves with God. *Willful attention, boundary creation*, and *fearless humility*, much like the monastic enclosure, create the space we need to orient ourselves toward the movement of the Spirit.

The second three practices focus on relationship. Since we are talking about social transformation and not just individual spiritual practice, we need to listen to Jesus' teachings on relationship. How do we transform relationships bounded by ego into relationships defined by love and compassion? *Self-awareness, powerful presence*, and *compassionate relationship* are stances that allow us to be with one another in new ways.

The third section turns to Jesus' teachings on money and our relationship to material goods. It is here that we can see most clearly the direct connection between spiritual practice and social transformation. Those of us involved in spiritual work should be suspicious of any spirituality that does not look at our relationship with the material world.

In America, we regularly see spirituality taught and practiced in upper class settings where the economic social location of both the practitioners and the setting are rarely even discussed, much less questioned. Fancy spas and retreat centers, many of which are in foreign destinations in poor countries, are commonplace in the world of spiritual teaching. Yet contemplative Christianity, as manifested in the monastic tradition, has always had an economic vision that coincides with the teachings in the Sermon on the Mount in which Jesus takes seriously the problems caused by our idolatrous relationship with money. The economic vision and model found in these communities was based upon communal work as a means of support, sharing of resources, and an understanding of "enough," often cast as a vow of poverty, which didn't mean destitution but rather practicing being content with having one's basic needs met.

Serving God, radical trust, and *letting go* are practices fundamental to reforming our relationship with material wealth and creating a just society.

The final three chapters bring into focus practices that directly engage our relationship to the world at large. *Discernment, loving your enemy,* and the overarching practice of *prayer,* all employ the previous practices to allow us and our communities to be agents of social transformation. With these practices, we will see how we may move with God into the world to, as we hear in that oft-quoted phrase of Martin Luther King Jr., bend the moral arc of the universe toward justice.

The Spiritual Life Is Always Aspirational

It's easy to become cynical and hopeless as we face the realities of the world and the history of humanity. Despite thousands of years of spiritual teachings, despite theological assertions of God's power and presence, despite the actions of millions of well-intentioned people, massive unnecessary suffering is the norm for a significant percentage of people. This is the inescapable truth.

Thus, it's important to realize that all teachings on spiritual life and practice are aspirational. As Jesus often said, the kingdom of God is both right here and not now. We have moments of realization, wakefulness, justice, and peace, and just as easily, these can vanish as if they never existed.

But this is why it's called *practice*. We, at least so far, never arrive. We just practice. We find others to practice with. And that's all. This brings us full circle to my comments about simple but not easy. The beloved community isn't something we build, achieve, or solidify; it's something we must practice over and over. It is my hope that this book can be a helpful guide on that journey.

Let us pray.

1

CREATING FOCUS IN MY LIFE
The Practice of Willful Attention

> *Enter through the narrow gate, for the gate is wide and the road is easy that leads to destruction, and there are many who take it. For the gate is narrow and the road is hard that leads to life, and there are few who find it.*
> —Matthew 7:13-14

Starting at the Beginning

A good description of the spiritual life is that it's an expression of our "intention to pay attention"—to pay attention to ourselves, to pay attention to others, to pay attention to our life. This book is about attending to the ordering of our life and the practices that help us live this life with God, a life that leads to a social transformation that reveals the beloved community. It is about how we do this work as individuals and collectively. If a group of people wishes to live a life with God, how might that happen? What are the habits and practices and examples within the Christian tradition that teach us the consistency of such a life?

As I mentioned in the introduction, our traveling companion on this journey is Jesus and his Sermon on the Mount. A quick reading shows that Jesus spends little time on doctrine or dogma. Rather, he is discussing how to live, how to relate to ourselves, to others, to God. This speech is so profound and so radical that, sadly, most Christians ignore it altogether, even if we hear it read in church a lot! What Jesus places before us seems impossible and even absurd. Yet we must use these teachings as the basis for our life together if we are to take our spiritual lives seriously. Jesus is our teacher, our spiritual leader, our God incarnate. Shouldn't we listen to him and at least try to follow?

In these first three chapters, we look at practices at the heart of living a life with God and examine how these practices reveal a society congruent with the divine will. While there are many types of spiritual practices, certain ones are foundational across the entire spectrum of contemplative prayer. The practice of silence is an example of a core practice. This first section explores practices that underlie and support the practices that follow. They inform everything about the way we engage our outward lives as followers of Jesus. The first, *willful attention*, continually orients our life. This is what Jesus describes in these two verses on the narrow gate.

This Life or the Next?

When we think about willful attention—a phrase that implies that we are trying to focus our mind—the immediate questions are "What are we attending to?" and "Where do we put our effort?" We need to spend some time looking at these questions in detail. Without clarity regarding these issues, we will immediately become lost on our journey.

As Christianity transformed from a movement into a religion, something that took several hundred years, adherents and teachers worked to define and clarify what was the point of becoming a Christian. People would logically want to know why they should convert to this new faith, and people in the faith wanted to explore and refine their own beliefs. Additionally, because Jesus himself wasn't physically present anymore, and because he wasn't returning out of the sky—at least it didn't appear that was happening any time soon—those who were in charge of this new religion were free to orient the teachings and the theology of Christianity however they wished, and Jesus wasn't there to correct them. As time went on, particularly in the fifth and sixth centuries CE, this work was done at the behest of the Roman emperors in service of their empire.

The various conferences and gatherings called by these emperors, which were largely focused on creating the theological statements that cast Jesus as a sky God—eventually one person of the Trinity—set in motion a trend whereby the afterlife became the focus of Christianity, and following Jesus became about what happens after we die. Even though the Hebrew Bible and the Christian scriptures have very little to say about an afterlife—but rather has a lot to say about what a just earthly kingdom looks like—those who were creating Christianity steadily forced Jesus' teachings into an after-death orientation.

Why might this happen? While there are undoubtably several reasons, two stand out to me as obvious and logical. First, if Jesus wasn't coming back to earth, a religion centered on him could easily become about going to wherever he was so that we could be with him. And if he was up in the heavenly realms, well then salvation looks like going up to be in heaven too.

Second, and more significant from the perspective of social transformation, a religion whose focus is on what happens to you after you die is a religion that the empire can use to control people and the social order. If you can convince people that an invisible sky God is watching how they behave and judging them on that behavior, then it's easy to scare people into submission. Such a population is exactly what suits the needs of an empire that wishes to maintain power over society. And anything in the Bible that appears to question the empire can simply be finessed to explain life after death or life after Jesus comes back at some unknown distant future time.

Looking back over the past 1,500 years of Christian history, this after-death focus has been incredibly effective and has achieved these aims and ends. Christians have had no problem committing all manner of atrocities and horrors for their imperial leaders in Jesus' name. And these Christian empires have effectively used Christianity as one of their tools for social control. When confronted with these issues, Christian leaders have regularly used some form of "pie in the sky when you die" theology to deflect the conversation away from issues of earthly justice and peace.

Today, even in churches that claim to have shed an exclusive focus on life after death, the most common understanding of Christianity and the work of Jesus is that he came so that we may have life eternal. This is so much a part of Christian formation that it's important to point it out and see it. Without such an awareness, we subconsciously and automatically read this orientation back into the Bible. Thus, when Jesus talks about the narrow gate and the path to life or destruction, most Christians think that he is talking about heaven and hell, even though Jesus doesn't say this in his talk or teachings.

While the Roman Empire was developing its form of Christianity, another form was appearing, the form which later was called the contemplative tradition or the tradition of the spiritual life. This Christianity was generally housed in monastic communities, but it also took alternative communal forms such as the Desert monastics or, much later, the Beguine communities in the Lowlands of northern Europe. This form of Christianity, while understanding that an eternal afterlife was an aspect of our faith, was primarily focused on the present kingdom of God. The Desert Mothers and Fathers created stories and sayings that to the modern American ear might sound like Zen koans. These teachings are all about contemplative life and how it brings us closer to

God. The afterlife is certainly a reality for these hermits, but their day-to-day life is focused on spiritual transformation. Reading the Bible without the constant overlay of heaven and hell, this tradition saw that God wished for a just kingdom on earth, not as a prerequisite for going to heaven, but rather as the main point of Jesus' teachings. It even says so right in the Lord's Prayer!

Unfortunately, this form of the faith has always been the minority report because it is a threat to whatever empire happens to be in charge at the time. For example, when Mary says that God has brought down the mighty and lifted up the lowly (see Luke 1:52), is she talking about on earth or after we die? The former threatens empire; the latter doesn't. The latter view leads to a reinforcement of society as it is—full of war and oppression—but the former facilitates social transformation. Obviously, those in charge of an unjust empire would rather have the second choice preached over the first. This is exactly what has happened repeatedly throughout history.

I've devoted a significant number of words to this issue because it's of great importance as we seek to practice Christianity and for what follows in this book in relation to social transformation. I cannot decide for you what is the "correct" form of Christianity. What I can do, however, is make clear my orientation and that of my teachers, living and dead. The spiritual life tradition has, in the main, understood Jesus to be talking about life on earth. The problem of human existence is here on this planet, not somewhere else in the sky. When we talk about the coming of God's kingdom, we are talking about human society becoming more just and peaceful. God's desire, the desire that Jesus is preaching, is for God's will to be done on earth as in heaven. So, when I talk about practices that create a life with God, I am not talking about practices that get us into heaven. I am talking about practices that transform life on earth. This is our focus and where we are called to put our effort.

The Narrow Gate: God at the Center

If the image of the wide and narrow gate isn't about going to heaven or hell, what then is Jesus describing? He is contrasting the life of habitual pattern—the life given to us by the world of ego, the world that's devoid of awareness, compassion, and love—with the life lived with God, the spiritual life.

As we look at history and the way that humans continue to function, we see that the way of destruction is easy. War and violence are endemic to the human experience. It doesn't take much to whip people up into a frenzy so that they will support an attack upon "the other," whoever that other may be. There are so many examples of this behavior and this pattern of action that it feels trivial to pick one. But, for clarity's sake, just look at the USA Federal Budget. For all of the supposed division and divisiveness in our political system, year after year, the two political parties join together to pass, almost without debate, an ever-increasing war budget that has now reached almost a trillion dollars a year, not including supplemental spending, which, as just one example, has reached over $6 trillion for the wars in Iraq and Afghanistan.[3] On this there is near complete agreement—the wide gate is full, easy, and well-funded.

The spiritual life teaches us that as we grow, we are formed by the habits and patterns given to us by society. One of the most powerful of these patterns is the will to survive. This is both an individual habit and a collective habit. Whether it is a small tribe, a feudal kingdom, or a nation-state, people identify with their "in group" and are then willing to protect this group at all costs. This is the easy road to destruction, and human beings walk it over and over and over again.

An essential aspect of such a path, of such a life, is that our spiritual practice is a secondary, add-on activity in our lives. Think about growing up in America. What is the one thing that parents drill into their children's heads repeatedly? "You have to get a job." The activities related to personal and communal survival are given greatest priority, and we carry this tendency into adulthood. I heard some version of, "Well I would do my spiritual practice, but I am too busy" so many times that I couldn't even guess the number.

By the time we reach adulthood, all our attention, energy, and focus are geared toward this activity of survival and personal accumulation, which we then feel justified in defending by any means necessary. We are trained into the path of destruction, and God—if God gets any time at all—is used to justify and validate our "goodness" and the life we are living.

Jesus contrasts this easy way taken by the majority with the way that is both hard and is also the way to life. I could not come up with a better way to describe the spiritual life. Spiritual practices are simple but not easy, yet they do indeed lead to a life full of the fruits of the Spirit, love, joy, peace, and justice. Why is this way so challenging and taken by so few? It stands in direct contrast and opposition to the easy highway of habit.

When we begin to focus our energy and effort toward our spiritual life, the first thing we notice is the suffering of the world. We notice our pain, our habitual patterns, and we become aware of the ways humans fail each other again and again. In short, we become aware of the world as it is and our part in it. This can be distressing, and it's very easy to return to the highway full of blissfully ignorant people running together down the road we all know. The biblical image of the people wanting to return to Egypt after fleeing to the desert is the classic image of our desire to return to the jail we know rather than face the wilderness we don't understand (see Exodus 16:1–12). Most monastic communities include a vow of stability because we often want to run.

Truly putting God and our spiritual life at the center of our activity is deeply unsettling. Our trust in this invisible being who, let's be honest, often seems more absent than present, is sorely tested. *If I am going to let go of the "easy" ways of my habitual patterns, then who am I? What is my path in life? What is in store for me?* These are just a few of the questions that arise and can cause us to become fearful and retreat from our practice.

Furthermore, society doesn't support people who devote their life energy to God and not to the whims of the powers that be in the world. As I discussed above, the empires of the world work to put habit and the wide way of destruction at the forefront of people's minds. They want society to remain the same, so they kill the prophets. Social transformation is what happens when groups of people begin to realign themselves and their energy toward this life with God. This threatens the status quo, and it requires great courage and effort.

Practicing God at the Center

So how do we enter this narrow gate? What does this mean on a practical level? The spiritual practice of willful attention comes down to issues of commitment and time, which really is another way of describing how we organize our lives. When we have made the commitment to a life with God, when we desire to engage in helping to manifest the beloved community, we begin to examine how our time is used and whether we have committed to our spiritual life and practice.

As I describe in my book *Creating a Life with God,* there are many different types of spiritual practice. Thus, when I talk about committing ourselves to our spiritual life and practice, I'm not saying that we must do twenty minutes of silent prayer a day, although certainly this is a great idea! Each of us, depending on our stage in life, our temperament, and our communal situation, will gravitate toward different practices. Some will prefer silence; some will spend more time with scripture; some will spend more time with nature. The issue isn't what we do as much as the fact that we do it.

In the Rule of St. Benedict, the term "work" is used to describe the prayer life of the monks. Manual labor isn't the work of the community but is something that you do when you are *not* working, when you are not praying. Imagine a reordering of your life and a commitment to adopt this perspective. What happens if you begin to see your life of prayer as your work and your other work as support for your life of prayer?

This new view begins to affect our schedule and how we order our time. I have talked with so many people who struggle to do their spiritual practice, and I always encourage them to put their prayer life on their calendar. Yet many of them resist this notion. This resistance reflects the "easy way" and a subconscious fear of the narrow gate. We know that things on our calendar get done. If we put our prayer life on our calendar, then it will happen, God will begin to form and shape us and our lives. Yet for most people, prayer is something that we get to if there is time, which, of course, there never is.

These descriptions of how we put our life with God at the center apply to groups that we are a part of as much as they do to individuals. What if church membership required being in a contemplative prayer group? Do we seek out others who wish to also put seeking the beloved community at the forefront of their lives? How do we organize our communal life around prayer?

As you begin your new journey of social transformation, start by taking an inventory of your commitments and your calendar. Begin to put times of prayer in regular slots. Begin to reorder your thinking to understand that your spiritual life is the at the center of your life. Invite this life and God into the center. As you do this, you enter the narrow gate, and your life and the life of your community will begin to change. Such transformation creates the need for new choices and boundary creation, the subject of the next chapter and the next teaching from Jesus' sermon.

2

WHERE DO I PUT MY EFFORT?
The Practice of Boundary Creation

Do not give what is holy to dogs, and do not throw your pearls before swine, or they will trample them under foot and turn and maul you.

—Matthew 7:6

The Call of Empire

If only the narrow gate were like the well that Alice fell into or the magic wardrobe that brought the children to Narnia. In these stories, the children are transported to another realm, and they stay there until they decide to return. But our lives don't work like that. The wide road to destruction is always there, always beckoning, and it's easy to get back on that road. Often it happens without us even knowing it. Anyone who has embarked upon the spiritual journey or any journey of growth or healing knows that we regularly find ourselves right back where we started. The habits of ego are powerful.

The practice in this chapter, boundary creation, helps address this issue of reverting to our habitual selves and is the next fundamental practice for social transformation. As was true with the narrow gate passage, this passage of pearls and swine, dogs and holiness has been misused. For as I talked about in chapter 1, the ways heaven-oriented Christianity has used these passages are often unhelpful or even harmful. If we are to hear something different, we must first acknowledge the images and ideas that come to mind automatically as we hear scripture. These preconceptions can prevent us from hearing the powerful, socially transformative message of Jesus.

This passage is most often used to be judgmental of others. We, the good Christians with the correct dogma and doctrine, are to protect ourselves from those who are swine and dogs. Such judgment takes many forms, whether it is about purity, or against another religion, or against other Christians with whom we disagree. What's tragic about such an interpretation of this teaching is that the passage directly follows several teachings about *not* being judgmental! It's almost as if Jesus were setting up this passage by warning people that he's not talking about judging others. Yet again, it is easy for a religion that participates in conquest and control to forget that admonition and go right ahead promoting the judgmental interpretation. Thus, although this passage isn't the likely source of the insult, Jesus' use of "dogs" has no doubt helped this become a favorite insult directed toward those we do not like or those we wish to consider subhuman.

So, let us try to look at this another way. We know that pigs were considered unclean within Hebraic Law, so the most likely reason that pigs would have been present in large quantities within Judea was to feed the Roman soldiers. The herd of pigs in the story of the demoniac is another example of Jesus using pigs as an image of the Roman occupation (see Mark 5:1-20). When Jesus needs a place to send the demons, he uses a nearby herd of swine who then kill themselves as a result of being possessed. This would have deprived the Romans of food, and this image helps reveal Jesus as one who is working against the powers of the oppressing empire.

Thus "swine" calls to mind the lure of empire, the lure of the world of habit, ego, and temporal power. And we are a part of this world! Just as we saw in the narrow gate passage, Jesus isn't talking about us against them. He is talking about two aspects of ourselves or two possible paths that we can take: the path of spiritual liberation and freedom versus the path of worldly power and oppression, a path in which we all participate. Even members of the oppressed class do. In modern America, so many White people claim that if they had been alive during the time of slavery or the time of Jim Crow, they would have been abolitionists or supporters of civil rights. Yet there is no evidence that this would be the case. At the time of his death, Martin Luther King Jr. was polling as the most hated man in America, and it took almost two hundred years from the beginning of the slave system for a significant percentage of White Americans to become anti-slavery.[4]

This participation with the system is simply a normal part of our fallen world, of the world of suffering and confusion. We all acquiesce to the power of the social systems in which we are raised. This is what we come to consider normal. It is the unexamined life with which most are content. In fact, when the Roman Empire began to collapse and withdraw from areas of Northern Europe, rather than cheer the exiting oppressors, many lamented the loss of the overlords, easily forgetting that these were the same people who had killed thousands of their fellow citizens during the original conquest.[5] Most people like pigs and dogs.

If we want to be part of the social transformation that leads to the beloved community, we must do something different. Since we do not have a magic wardrobe that can transport us away or a starship to beam up to, we must again apply intention and awareness to form a different way of being in this world, the only one we have. Jesus isn't calling us to judge others in this passage; he is calling us to set the boundaries needed to live a life with God. The swine and dogs are not other people; they are the ideas and habits and distractions of the empire.

We Are Finite Beings

How many commercials and social commentaries have we seen that tell us we can have it all? And how many people, ourselves included, do we see running around over-scheduled, trying to squeeze one more experience or activity into our lives? I and some others have been talking for decades about the overuse of our time and the lack of Sabbath, yet these admonitions and teachings have fallen on deaf ears. I frequently talk with parents who lament not having much of a relationship with their kids, even as they schedule another activity that happens over dinner time, depriving them of the chance to eat and talk together.

Then within the corporate world, the newest tag line, as it becomes harder and harder to squeeze profits in this era of late-stage capitalism, is that workers must "do more with less." Electronic offices and the work-from-home reality created by the COVID-19 pandemic, both of which are often promoted as being a convenience, have mostly resulted in more time working, not less. Now we are plugged in 24/7. Everyone expects a reply to their email or text within five minutes. Many are doing the job of three or four people. And so, our time is squeezed by our own ideas about what we think we should be doing and by what the social structures of the kingdoms of the world are telling and forcing us to do. This reality creates tragic and paradoxical situations. Despite being overly busy and in need of vacations, every year the American workforce leaves over 700 million vacation days unused.[6] We clearly are confused about our boundaries as they relate to our time and our energy.

One of the hardest things for people to understand is that we are finite. The story of the Tower of Babel is about our refusal to understand our finitude (see Genesis 11:1-9). Humanity tries to build a tower to the sky so people can hang out with God. But we are finite creatures. This is why we need to attend to our time and our space.

The material world can exist and bring forth life because of boundaries, and boundaries are what mark our finite reality. The cell wall creates the container that holds the information and energy production that make the cell do what it does. The atmosphere creates a boundary between earth and space so that living creatures can exist on the planet's surface. In Genesis 1, we hear about the creation of the boundaries that hold back the waters so land can form. Gravity allows massive structures to create the bounded equilibrium systems we call planetary orbits. We even have the expression, "Good fences make good neighbors," a statement about the value of boundaries.

Similarly, our lives are ordered by many boundaries, most of which are given to us and of which we are frequently unaware. Language, culture, family history, genetics, nation, and social class all impose boundaries upon us. These are the boundaries of the kingdoms of the world, and we give our holiness, our image of God in which we are formed to the dogs of war and imperial rulers. In return, they trample upon us, taking our energy, our time, our humanity. When Jesus uses these images, he is not describing the relationship between good and bad people; he is describing the experience we all go through in the material world.

The spiritual life helps us become conscious of the boundaries we've been given. As I've said, these are the habits of our ego process. The activity of our life causes us to reinforce these boundaries over and over again. As we repeat these habits, we continue to give away what is holy in us. Jesus is calling us into a different kingdom. However, because we are finite beings, we cannot create the new boundaries needed for the kingdom of God without giving up at least some of the boundaries of the kingdoms of the earth. This is another reason why people have a hard time giving attention to their spiritual lives. In the first chapter, we saw how the practice of willful attention helps us redirect our attention; here we are seeing that another issue is the practice of boundary creation.

The Monastery Wall

Why does a monastery need a wall? This isn't a trivial question. When I lived and worked at a monastery, there were many people, my parents included, who were quite offended by the locked gate and fence around the monastery complex. Why do you need this fence if you are about openness, meditation, and compassion? "Very peaceful," said one person quite sarcastically.

The monastery wall is a symbol of the communal process of new boundary creation happening within the monastery. As the life of contemplation allows the members of the community to align the boundaries within their hearts, minds, and lives to the movement of the Spirit, the wall around the monastery reminds them and those outside the monastery of the need for this boundary formation.

Sometimes, people object to the language of the spiritual life that talks about the *world* and *the life of God*. "Don't we say that God is everywhere?" is often how the objection is framed. This is also an important issue. Yes indeed, God is everywhere. However, human beings are generally not attended to God's presence. We are absorbed in the life of the individual and collective egos of those with whom we share our social existence.

One of my favorite activities is kayaking on the rivers of northern Minnesota, especially the Red Lake River, which runs near the retreat center we manage. When the river is running high, it's wonderful to head downstream and paddle with the current. But if I try to go upstream, it's a lot of work, sometimes even impossible. No matter how hard I paddle, I go backward in the swollen river current. This is a great analogy for our lives in relation to God and ego. In our normal life situation, the flow of ego in our life is like the swollen river. Yes, we may have the ability and desire to paddle upstream to align ourselves with the way of the Divine, but the current is mostly too strong. We must, somehow, get out of the river and put our energy to use in situations where we can make progress. This act is what the boundary of the monastery wall symbolizes. It's not that God isn't everywhere, it's that we are in a situation, the condition of the flow of habitual pattern, where we cannot make headway in our life with God without some intentional actions that put us in another relationship with our lives.

This doesn't mean that we all need to lock ourselves away in monasteries, although this might not be a bad idea, but it does mean that we need to do something about the boundaries in our lives. Much of the work I do with people involves discussions about relationships with systems that are sucking the life out of them. Dysfunctional family systems, work systems, social systems, and relationships with various substances are all defined by boundaries that are often far more harmful than helpful. Yet suggesting a change in these relationships is frequently met with protests that such changes are impossible.

When we consider making these changes, we are often met with a flood of internal and external responses that are designed by the systems themselves to keep us in line. We feel guilt; we face emotional manipulation, criticism, internal and external voices telling us we are selfish, ungrateful, bad children, bad workers, on and on. This assault is powerful, painful, and highly effective. It is the gravitational pull of the old boundaries, and much of the time, our little spaceship, trying to vault into a different realm, crashes back into the ground, firmly rooting us in our old lives.

This is why we call spiritual practice, *practice*. To move into a new way of being, we need to launch ourselves again and again, each time we have more power to break free into a new realm.

Practicing New Boundaries

Like all practices, the spiritual practice of boundary creation begins with paying attention to our life and honestly assessing the nature of our current boundary situations. Most of you reading this have likely been on a spiritual retreat of some kind. A retreat is a period of new boundary creation. We take time to pray; we take time to walk; we slow down; we turn off our cell phones. After a few days, or even a few hours, we feel different. We are more relaxed; we breathe; we feel at peace; even the colors around us appear more vivid. If a group goes on retreat for a long time, at least a month, people even begin to look different as their muscles relax.

The practice of boundary creation mimics the process of a retreat: We begin to shift what we give our pearls and our holiness—our time, our presence, our selves—to. To do this, we must recognize our inherent value and the value of our time and presence. One of the ways the boundaries of the world keep us trapped is by convincing us that we lack pearls and holiness. I often ask people if they ever consider that being with them is an incredible gift and that people are lucky when they get to spend time with them. Almost one hundred percent of the time, this thought has never crossed their minds. If you do not believe you have any pearls or holiness to give, you do not worry about wasting them!

As we begin to recognize the value we carry as a being formed in God's image, we slowly develop the courage and desire to shift the boundaries in our lives. In the addiction-recovery world, it is said that as we embrace sobriety, we need to change "people, places, and activities." This is essentially a commitment to new boundaries. We are all addicted to the habits given to us by the world. Social transformation, creating a life with God, requires that we embrace a new way of ordering the world.

But we do not do this alone. The monastery isn't inhabited by one person but by a community. Thus, not only do we begin to ask ourselves what new boundaries we need, but we also begin to seek others who want a socially transformed spiritual life, and we begin to create new life with these new communities.

Some of the specific questions to consider as part of your boundary practice are the following:

Are there individuals or groups of people you expend a lot of time and energy on who are just trampling your pearls?

Are there social systems you are involved with that amplify your holiness who are working with you and alongside you to develop your collective spiritual life?

How is your time used? What are the things you need to let go of? Do more of?

Do you spend time with people who value or de-value you? What human boundaries do you need to change?

What reminders would help you create these new boundaries? Do you need lists posted on your bathroom mirror? Reminders on your phone? A person who serves as an accountability partner?

As you ask and practice answering these questions, you will notice your life starting to change. You may notice more energy, greater depth in your relationships, activities that are more worthwhile and satisfying. You may find that you are involved in new activities that change your community. You are a part of the social transformation that God desires.

This moves us more fully into a life with God and begins to arouse in us fearless humility, our next fundamental practice.

3

WHO IS BLESSED?
The Practice of Fearless Humility

When Jesus saw the crowds, he went up the mountain, and after he sat down, his disciples came to him. And he began to speak and taught them, saying:

"Blessed are the poor in spirit, for theirs is the kingdom of heaven.

"Blessed are those who mourn, for they will be comforted.

"Blessed are the meek, for they will inherit the earth.

"Blessed are those who hunger and thirst for righteousness, for they will be filled.

"Blessed are the merciful, for they will receive mercy.

"Blessed are the pure in heart, for they will see God.

"Blessed are the peacemakers, for they will be called children of God.

"Blessed are those who are persecuted for the sake of righteousness, for theirs is the kingdom of heaven.

"Blessed are you when people revile you and persecute you and utter all kinds of evil against you falsely on my account. Rejoice and be glad, for your reward is great in heaven, for in the same way they persecuted the prophets who were before you."
—Matthew 5:1-12

Paradoxical Blessing

The practices of the first two chapters create the environment for our life with God. We are focused; we have boundaries, now what? What happens in this space that allows for the transformative work of the Spirit? What do we encounter in our new environment that is "holy" and facilitates transformation? The logical answer would be God. However, relating to God is not a magical event that happens without our active participation. This is why we are doing spiritual practices. Once we are in a position where we can engage more fully with the Divine Spirit, we still need to have a basic stance, an approach through which we can listen for and experience God. In this chapter, we examine fearless humility, our third fundamental practice and the one that grounds us in our holy environment.

WHO IS BLESSED?

Most traditions use a word that translates as "blessing" to describe the result of an encounter with God. We are blessed when we meet the life-giving Spirit. But what is "blessing"? How do we define it, see it, experience it? While blessing is a term that may begin with a deeper spiritual meaning—in the Christian tradition this might be talked about as taking on the mind of Christ for example (see 1 Corinthians 2:16)—it eventually becomes defined as worldly success. I am blessed by God if I have money, winning, fame, power. Part of this impulse is natural; life is hard, and people want God to help them live a better, easier life. However, this natural human desire for help can far too often morph into a runaway desire for endless consumption and power.

I recently had an online conversation about the practice of thanking God for a sports victory, a habit that I find both annoying and problematic. Some who responded to my reflection argued that it wasn't necessarily a sign of problematic theology but just something said in the excitement of the moment. I can certainly appreciate that perspective, but I noted that I have never seen anyone giving God the glory and thanking God for a loss on national television.

The hashtag "#blessed" has become popular recently in the United States, and this also carries with it a similar slant. People are blessed with good health, a good family, or a good material situation. And although there are some who have recognized how problematic this idea is and make fun of the term, I often hear people talking about being blessed in contrast to those who have little in the way of material goods. While I have nothing against gratitude or appreciating what we have (this is a very good practice), we need to admit that there is a long history of the empires of the world thinking and promoting the idea that blessing equals material prosperity and success, always at the expense of other human beings.

I believe that this is why Jesus begins his sermon with a statement on blessing that is paradoxical and antithetical to this traditional, imperial, notion of blessing. If we are going to look at spiritually driven social transformation that ushers in the beloved community, then we need to understand this core religious concept *blessing* differently. And one clear sign that his statements are radical and threatening to empire is that they, like all the other passages we are going to travel with in this book, have been changed from plain statements about this world into harmless promises about the heaven that awaits us after death.

An interpretation of the Beatitudes that focuses on heaven fits perfectly with the after-death orientation of Christianity I've described above. This common perspective assumes that the "will be" statements of the blessings refer to a time after death. This view fits with the understanding of how blessing works on earth. If blessing is about success, then a blessing that doesn't lead to success here must be describing a success that happens in another realm. Persecution can't be blessing; victory is blessing! So, Jesus must be talking about blessing after we die. And yet, he doesn't say this. Rather, Jesus says that those experiencing states of being we usually consider the opposite of blessings are both blessed now and in the future. Viewed from a material-world perspective, as opposed to using the after-death sleight-of-hand trick, this new blessing dynamic describes both the process of creating a new society and the nature of the future society God desires. Blessing in this sense is part of the process of moving toward that society. Those who are seriously engaged in social transformation, who are putting their lives on the line for something different, are helping to create that blessed, vastly different, future. In that process, they are blessed as well.

Looking at the rest of the sermon and Jesus' life, we see that Jesus radically redefines blessing. A blessing is not a thing or a result. It is not something that the empire could give, even if it wanted to. To be blessed is to follow Jesus in creating the beloved community. This present and process-oriented view is how the Christian spiritual tradition has chosen to understand blessing. This understanding leads to this chapter's practice: fearless humility.

Humility: The First Rung of the Ladder

One metaphor for the spiritual life that's been popular over the centuries is a ladder leading to God (see Genesis 28:12). This of course comes from the common notion that heaven is "up," so you may not resonate with this stairway-to-heaven concept! However, climbing a ladder is like walking a path in that it is something we do to move step by step toward our destination. It is an image of movement and growth.

Each rung in this metaphor is a practice or a posture that we take to progress, and humility is usually considered the first, most essential, step. Without humility, we make little progress. So, what is the connection between Jesus' list of paradoxical blessings and humility?

In our modern era, especially within the workaholic United States, there are few greater insults than to be called "ineffective." In our work, in our personal life, in our relationship with God, society says that we must have a purpose and goals so we can be effective in "operationalizing" those activities that get us to success. Within this environment, "coaching," a modality whose focus is on helping us to reach our goals, has resonated deeply with people who want someone to help them progress toward their best life. We are indeed to be masters of the universe!

The manifestations of this ruthless drive are everywhere. We are a society with deep ambivalence—bordering on hatred—about the poor, those who are sick or disabled, and anyone who seems to be unable to pull themselves up by their bootstraps and succeed. In addition, we are amid an epidemic of anxiety and depression, auto-immune diseases, and pain, all of which are manifestations of an endless desire to be better and better, a brutal march of judgment and self-flagellation.

The idea that we could be blessed by being involved with peacemaking, which on the face of it will fail again and again, is a basic heresy in a society addicted to effective results. We could go down the list of the Beatitudes and see this ineffectiveness repeated with each one. As just another example, consider mourning. When someone in our life dies, the messages we receive are that we should be fine, get over it, and move on. Taking time off work, taking time to grieve in community is both actively and passively discouraged. The blessing is that we can get back on our feet, not that we are mourning.

The theological problem lurking behind our addiction to results is the ancient idea that we, mere creatures, are in fact God. This is another aspect of the Tower of Babel confusion I mentioned in the last chapter. We are not infinite beings. We are created creatures. Just as our time and space are limited, so too is our power. Humility is the practice of returning again and again to the truth of our limitations. We recognize that saving the world—creating the present kingdom—is not our job. We cannot manage our own way to the beloved community. Blessing, the deep encounter with the Spirit with whom we cooperate in social transformation, arises as we let go of our need to control and our delusion that we are tasked with fixing everything. Humility prepares us for actions that the world derides and deems ineffective because they run counter to our enslavement by the empire.

Some of you may be old enough to remember the original promise of the computer: It was going to save us time. We were going to be able to work less and have more free time for the good things of life. We have been scammed. Instead of freeing time, the computer has become a way for us to work all the time! Now there is even less time for the things of our life with God. This is why the first two practices were so important: We must create communities of practice that begin to live in the way of humility. But before we go deeper into what the spiritual practice of fearless humility is, we must discuss what humility is *not*.

Fearful Versus Fearless Humility

Like all spiritual teachings and concepts, humility is a notion that can be deployed in a manner that is healthy or unhealthy. If an organization is trying to control its population, teaching them to be docile and not pay attention to their wants and needs is a wonderful technique to achieve its aims. Unfortunately, religion often functions this way. I cannot count the number of people I have worked with who think that paying attention to their inner voices of desire and wisdom is "selfish."

Humility is often characterized as "false" or "true" humility to distinguish between these helpful and unhelpful forms of the practice. Here I prefer to use the terms "fearful" or "fearless" humility because I think that these modifiers more accurately reflect the spiritual issue behind these two ways of understanding the term.

Humility that arises out of fear is unhelpful. Our understanding of theologically related ideas arises, consciously or subconsciously, from our image of God. Imperial Christianity has leaned heavily upon what I like to describe as the "psychotic warlord" image of God, meaning that God the Father is in charge and will mete out punishment to all for disobedience. In its most extreme case, this punishment is given even to those who have never heard of Jesus or Christianity or salvation. This image is so common that when I worked in a program for men who'd practiced domestic violence, most of the men identified Christian theology as justification for their violence: If God was in charge of the world and punished violently, then men, who were in charge of the household, could also use violence as punishment. If humans are little more than worms who are evil sinners and God is an angry tyrant who is going to send us to hell for any small transgression, then the natural response to such an invisible divine being is fear. This is not the fear of the Lord described in the Wisdom tradition; rather it is the fear of trauma. It is the fear of a child brutalized by an abusive parent.

Under such conditions, humility is simply cowering in the dust, bent over, face down, hoping against hope that you are going to be ignored and passed over so as not to be punished. In this state, you try to suppress every desire, every want, every need, because you are sure you are not humble enough, but are bad, and your faith is simply about wishing that you had done the right things needed to get into heaven.

This approach to faith and God is one that causes what has recently been labeled *religious trauma*.[7] Although not yet a formal psychological diagnosis, the trauma associated with frequent childhood exposure to this sort of faith is becoming widely recognized as contributing to a constellation of reactions similar to post-traumatic stress disorder (PTSD). Clearly, such a fearful humility isn't valuable or consistent with the best spiritual teachings of our faith.

By contrast, fearless humility arises from very different images of God and ourselves. The word *humility* comes from the Latin word *humus* and refers to connection with the earth. From dust we have come and to dust we shall return (see Genesis 3:19). We are created beings, not God, and we recognize this not as something to fear, but rather as a fact of our created reality. Far from being a psychotic warlord, God is revealed in Jesus, who loves and lifts up, heals and forgives.

Humility arises from a poverty of spirit, which simply means that we are enlivened and made well by the Holy Spirit, not a spirit of our ego selves. And we are fearless because we are aligned with God. It is not that we never feel afraid; it is that our spiritual lives ground us in an eternal divine connection.

Humility from this perspective doesn't disconnect us from who we are, the hallmark of fearful humility, but rather allows us to be fully ourselves. The good image of God that lies within us can emerge as we tend to who God has created us to be. The paradox of humility is that fearless humility results in our becoming our most empowered human selves.

An outstanding historical example of this truth is Catherine of Siena. She lived in the fourteenth century in what is now Italy and was born the twenty-third of twenty-four children. Despite being illiterate, she is credited as being one of the first European women to publish a book and was an ambassador for Pope Gregory IX, of whom she was also a fierce critic. She was canonized in 1461 and was the second woman given the title of Doctor of the Church, in 1970. Yet the outstanding feature of her letters and essays, which generally begin with the phrase, "I Catherine a servant and slave of Jesus" was her great humility and her absolute reliance on God.[8]

Catherine is indeed a portrait of humility in the best sense of the word. She was fearless and resolute in her work and calling, and she never lost sight of the Divine Spirit that animated and guided her work.

This is the humility to which we are called in the upside-down world of blessing. How do we make this an active practice as we seek social transformation?

Humility and Spiritual Freedom

Humility is usually described as a passive state. I am humble, and therefore I sit quietly or I don't take up too much space or I don't share my ideas and suggestions. These are all qualities of the fearful humility described above. Remember that fearless humility is the first rung of the ladder of the spiritual life. As such, humility is an active practice, and this is why it's appearing here in a book about social transformation.

Humility as a practice is closely aligned with the notion of spiritual freedom. As the members of the new contemplative communities began to gather and live together during the period of their formation in the early sixth century, they found that their reliance on God freed them from the constraints of the social norms of the Empire. Within their bounded communities, they could now live as God was calling them, as transformed people creating the beloved community.

So, fearless humility frees us to act in the world in new and different ways. It is the opposite of a cowering person afraid of an angry God. Again, paradoxically, the humble person enlivened by the Spirit is active, playful, fierce, and deeply engaged with the community, but not in a way that dominates and controls.

Humility as a practice also opens us to curiosity about others and about what God is doing in the world. In the "normal" hierarchical world of blessing, only those who are the most famous and successful are interesting and worthy of attention. This is why so many people spend their lives comparing themselves to others in a negative light, always finding themselves falling short, full of inadequacies.

Yet we know that we are all at the same time dust and formed in God's image. Humility allows us to let go of this toxic view of human value and begin to appreciate each person. In our community, we become increasingly interested in the life of every member, we see an entire universe in each human life, and we are in awe of the manifest ways that God's image enters the world. This practice alone is socially transforming. The field of positive childhood experiences shows the great value of every adult who takes an interest in a child and how these experiences, no matter how difficult the child's situation, increase their chance of living a healthy life.[9] Now imagine if every person was shown loving interest and attention! This is what happens in a community that practices fearless humility. All are appreciated; all gifts are honored; all are seen as bearers of God's spirit as each is freed to be a loving presence to one another.

The practice of fearless humility thus proceeds through several steps that are repeated throughout our lives. These are steps both for an individual and a community.

We begin by seeking to free ourselves from any unhelpful or toxic views about humility.

We then engage the realization that we are both dust and created in God's image. We align ourselves as creatures and not creators. This is done through active reflection on who we are as human beings.

Our ongoing spiritual practice allows us to become more aware of God's spirit moving in our lives. We notice an increase in compassion, in curiosity about others, and in the world around us.

We continue to look for signs and experiences of freedom in our lives and in the life of our community. Where are we called to be of service, of witness, and forces for social transformation?

As we come to the close of these first three chapters, we have set the stage for the next set of practices for social transformation, practices that focus on relationships in the beloved community. The fundamental practices discussed so far have created the environment for living in a new way. We have oriented our time around our spiritual life; we have created a bounded environment within which we can practice with our community; and we have humbly aligned ourselves with the world of upside-down blessing so that we can freely engage life according to the movement of the Spirit. Now let us move to a deeper awareness of how we relate to the world and those around us.

4

USING OUR GOOD EYE
The Practice of Self-Awareness

Do not judge, so that you may not be judged. For the judgment you give will be the judgment you get, and the measure you give will be the measure you get. Why do you see the speck in your neighbor's eye but do not notice the log in your own eye? Or how can you say to your neighbor, "Let me take the speck out of your eye," while the log is in your own eye? You hypocrite, first take the log out of your own eye, and then you will see clearly to take the speck out of your neighbor's eye.
—Matthew 7:1-5

Relationship Practices

In the first three chapters, I discussed practices to create an environment where communities and individuals can work with the Spirit, allowing the beloved community to appear. Whenever we act in the world, we need an environment conducive to what we are trying to do. Teachers need classrooms; carpenters need workshops; doctors need hospitals. Transformed humans need a "monastery," an environment for spiritual practice. So, we focus our lives; we create needed boundaries, and we become fearlessly humble. Now what?

In the next three chapters, we will discuss relationship practices. Jesus' ministry was one of relationships. As those around Jesus engaged with him, their interactions became the substrate for his teachings, a series of object lessons that reveal the heart of God. He doesn't just talk about how God wants us to relate to people with leprosy; he provides examples of what God desires.

This is more than just "teaching by example." To explain what is happening, I need to explain the process by which we become "ourselves"—the process of the formation of our sense of self or the "ego-process."

The human ego-process—and I use this term *process* so that we understand that the ego isn't a static thing in our heads but a pattern formed over and over again—is the normal set of mental activities that makes us into functional human beings in the world. This process relies on the creation of dualities, the primary one being "self" and "other." To be aware that I am an individual, I must be aware of myself as separate from the rest of the world. This is true about every aspect of ourselves. We need to know what is "ours" and what is "the world's."

Our minds are skilled at this process. It happens automatically and is necessary for us to exist in the material world. From the moment we are born, and perhaps even a bit before that, every human brain is sorting things into three categories: *things I like, things I dislike,* and *things I ignore.* This sorting helps us make sense of the world and evaluate the incredible amount of information that is always coming to us through our senses.

By the time we are teenagers, we have a well-developed sense of ourselves as individuals as well as a vast array of preferences regarding the world. These are both internal and external. It is important to understand that these feelings about self and other are not static entities that are created in our brain and then left alone; rather, the mind is perpetually at work repeating and reinforcing our preferences. Every time we encounter any stimuli, and this happens literally millions of times a day, our mind sorts them into the "like," "dislike," and "ignore" categories, attempting to create a stable view of ourselves and the rest of reality. One of the implications of this process is that it makes us believe that new things are impossible by screening them out of our consciousness.

Today the idea of reprogramming our neurons is quite popular and well known. Search "reprogramming your brain" on Google and you'll get millions of self-help references. This idea is a modern image of the ancient contemplative truth that our spiritual practice can dissolve our ego structure and open our awareness to other possibilities. Although people are good at ignoring evidence that stares them in the face, there is truth to the saying, "Seeing is believing." Jesus demonstrates that new relational activities are possible, and he does so in the hope that we will practice them ourselves.

Perhaps the need for relational practices, like all spiritual practices, sounds obvious, but the evidence shows that isn't true. How many times do we find it necessary to say that a church community is full of "nice" people? How many times do we see a heartwarming relationship story in the news, not even pausing to recognize that it's in the news because it is the exception that proves the rule? There is something deeply flawed in the ways we relate to ourselves and others. Yet like any other undertaking of the human mind, we are capable of infinite delusion. Do we really think that there's no connection between the fact that people in the Upper Midwest of the United States boast so much about their great family relationships yet also have the highest binge drinking rates in the United States? How many drinks does it take to get through all those family gatherings?[10]

Jesus gives us multiple teachings about relationships in the Sermon on the Mount, but we will focus on the three that are the most basic and essential for creating a new society: self-awareness, powerful presence, and compassionate relationship.

Do You Hear Yourself?

One of my sons is a violinist, so I have spent a lot of time at violin lessons. I remember one of his teachers would exhort the students in the orchestra to listen to themselves as they played. When I first heard this, which again may sound obvious, it brought me back to my one horribly failed attempt at playing the violin. My elementary school offered group violin lessons because we didn't have any regular music program. We all stood in a circle with the violins given to us by the teacher, and we were told to play on one of the open strings. After about thirty seconds, I could hear that someone was playing a higher note than most of the class. It took me another thirty seconds or so to figure out that I was that student! Listening to ourselves doesn't happen automatically.

If I had to point to one place in scripture to prove the point that spiritual practice is simple but not easy, it would be the passage for this chapter. Just don't judge. Easy, right? How many times have we heard sermons on this passage from a church system that relentlessly judges everyone in the pews and everyone outside the church? In this short teaching, Jesus is pointing to a relational practice that lies at the heart of almost all spiritual practices: self-awareness. This is the spiritual equivalent of musicians listening to themselves. Do we hear who we are?

Jesus' use of a physical example—the log and the speck—to teach about a psycho-spiritual reality illustrates the challenge of hearing ourselves. When working with people, I also use physical examples to highlight the difficulty of psychological and spiritual change. For example, let's say that someone is dealing with a psychologically abusive family system. Now let's reframe the situation. If someone hit you with a stick every time you went to visit your family, most people would realize that you should not go visit them. Yet people feel compelled to continue to visit family who belittle, criticize, and traumatize them, and we don't consider that behavior to be particularly problematic, even though it's the same dynamic and does as much damage.

We can see and understand different issues when they are in the physical realm, but seeing our identities and our psychological habits is far harder. If we did literally walk around with a log in our eye, it wouldn't take long for us to remove the log.

This blindness, this lack of "eyes to see and ears to hear," comes from the nature of the ego development process itself. As we grow, forming an identity is one of the main tasks of the human mind. We cannot really see or understand this identity as a separate substance without practice. This is why listening to ourselves is one of the great tasks of the spiritual life. It is an activity that strengthens our awareness and then allows us to see ourselves from a new, outside, greater perspective.

We have all experienced a relational conflict where we are talking past each other. Every move in the debate is designed to shore up a position instead of creating deeper understanding. This is the ego process blocking self-awareness. In the language of the three-part sorting system, we are putting the new information into the "ignore" category and the person with whom we disagree into the "dislike" category. In short, we are defending ourselves against experiencing a new view because we know how shocking it can be to see ourselves from the outside and how such vision disrupts our tightly held beliefs. People who are caught doing something bad, illegal, or problematic, often suddenly see their behavior from an outside perspective and feel a tremendous amount of shame and horror.

On a much more benign note, many people, including myself, don't like hearing our recorded voice because it sounds so different from the outside than it does in our head. These experiences of shock at being seen point to the insular nature of the world of our ego-self: This is the giant log in our eye. This insularity is one of the main obstacles to the flowering of the kingdom of God because it isolates us all in our little ego-bubbles, where our primary focus is the preservation of our world. Thus, it isn't surprising that overcoming this isolation is one of the main purposes of spiritual life in community.

Judging as the Key Obstacle to Self-Awareness

If the ego were a castle, then the process of judging would be the moat, the castle wall, and the huge door blocking the entrance. Judging is the first and most important activity protecting our identity and our ego-habits. These judgments, which we have by the thousands, are mostly about small things. Every day, we go through life completing the sentence, "I am the person who [likes, dislikes, ignores] X."

When we read this Bible passage, however, we tend to hear *judgment* in a big way. We think of morals or eternal life or the latest issue in the culture war. But the teachings of the spiritual life go much deeper than that. Judging is a basic part of being human in the world, which is the world of empire. From the moment we are born, we are taught what is appropriate and inappropriate in our culture and family. When we enter school, we are taught all the things that are good, bad, cool, and uncool, right answers and wrong answers. Our life is situated in a constant stream of judgment.

This judging world then becomes full of separation, alienation, and violence. Communities and societies form around common cultural judgments, and these are the corporate egos of the principalities and powers. Tribes, nation-states, and empires are founded on judging themselves to be good and right and others to be less good and wrong and inferior. The language of colonialism is the language of judgment. People who were not of the European ruling class, and later who were not White, were deemed "savages" or "uncivilized" or only partly human.

All this behavior is, again, designed to keep a view of the world stable and promote an agenda or a particular preferred experience of life. So, the world of the ego is the world of constant moral judgment. It is this deeper, all-pervasive nature of our world that Jesus is trying to get us to see. Judging and being judged is our life, and God wishes it to be transformed into a life of self-awareness and love.

The Practice of Self-Awareness

When we begin our time of spiritual practice, whether it be silent prayer or some other type of prayer practice, some of the first things we encounter are our judgments. These are often quite harsh and directed at ourselves. *I'm not doing this right. I'm not good at this. Maybe I should be doing something else. It looks like that person across the room is better at this than I am.* Self-awareness begins with an awareness of our judging mind, which is powerful, well-trained, and continuously active.

People usually respond to this judging process by agreeing with it, participating internally in the judgment, or trying to ignore, suppress, or avoid it. One of the main reasons people find spiritual practices challenging is that it is hard and painful to encounter our own judgmentalism. Yet one of the main activities of the practice of prayer is to be able to sit with our mind—judgments and all—without running or feeding the judgments. We observe; we are curious, and we then let them go. This method of observation relies on curiosity rather than judgment. It is what Jesus is describing when he asks us to look with an eye that is free of logs, a good eye.

This process of observation is the first step in the formation of a new relationship with ourselves that will then blossom into a new relationship with others. It is how self-awareness is a powerful transformative social practice. The spiritual life slowly begins to replace judgment with curiosity. Those who have spent any time around kids know that they are endlessly curious. From grabbing things and putting them in their mouths, to exploring what might happen if they swing this stick around, to picking up everything they can reach in the room, curiosity drives their learning and development. They have no sense that it's wrong to eat dirt, draw on the walls, or laugh at any silly thing they see.

Yet by the time a curious child reaches adulthood, that curiosity has been regularly suppressed and replaced with judgment. In many people, curiosity has disappeared altogether. When we hear that we must become like a child to enter the kingdom of God, replacing judgment with curiosity is one of the major transformations required for this shift in relationship with the world around us.

Just as judgment is the vanguard of ego, curiosity is the path to self-awareness, yet over the course of our life, we display little interest in becoming curious about who we are. When teaching about spiritual practices and contemplative psychology, I often point out that we know when children do something and we ask them why, they often say, "I don't know," which perhaps we would consider normal for young children whose brains are still developing. Yet if you ask those same people forty years later why they act a certain way, you will often get that same reply: "I don't know." Nothing much seems to have changed on the self-reflection front. Self-awareness is the process of coming to know who we are, and it requires that we become endlessly curious about ourselves and our lives. As we reflect upon our life's journey, we come to know what has formed us and what we are attached to. We discover the repetitive judgments we make about ourselves and others, and this knowledge frees us to begin to make true choices in our lives, not out of reactive judgment but out of clarity and care. The log is gone from our eyes, and we can see the path we would walk in the world.

Community and Power Dynamics

This self-awareness isn't practiced in isolation. We are talking about practices that create social transformation toward the beloved community, and self-awareness creates the conditions for transformed relationships. While the practice of self-awareness may begin with curiosity about my own mind in isolation from others, it soon develops into a curiosity about others and how I relate to others. I can start to be curious about my reactions to certain people and certain groups of people. Whom do I avoid and toward whom do I gravitate? Whom do I judge because of their look, their clothes, their speech? Why do I do these things?

As I let go of my judging mind, I can develop an interest in myself in relation to the world. And those with whom I am in community are practicing the same thing in relation to me. Rather than being a group of ego-filled adults reinforcing their judgments of themselves, one another, and the world around them, we become a community of curious seekers desiring to love and be loved.

In society, one of the most toxic manifestations of judgment is the creation of unequal power dynamics in the social order. Those who are judged to be "good" or "the right kind of people" are given more power, while those who are "bad" are oppressed. It also works the other way when those who take or have power become those who are labeled "good" in the social structure, while those who have little power are considered "bad." One of the best examples of this in the United States is that those who are poor are regularly seen as lazy, even though many of the working poor are the hardest working people in a society that simply doesn't pay them a living wage. Communal self-awareness reveals these imbalances and allows those who are more powerful to give up their unequal position while those who are less powerful can become empowered, as we saw in the spiritual practice of fearless humility.

Racism in the USA is one of the best examples of how judgment leads to massive power imbalances and a society that needs holy transformation. White people have a very hard time seeing their power and the judgments that help maintain their position. The practice of self-awareness—individual and communal—is essential for overcoming and transforming these imbalances and injustices. We can convert Mary's speech into powerful spiritual practice questions: *If I am of the mighty in society, how can I come down? And if I am of the lowly, how can I rise up?*

The process of community self-awareness also reveals a second tragic aspect of life in the fallen world: Most of the judgments that we think are important and cling to tightly don't matter at all. Imprisonment by the trivial is another way the kingdoms of the world prevent us from manifesting the kingdom of God.

As we develop our own self-awareness and our good eye, we come to see the world not as place full of right and wrong, good or bad, but a place of endless variety and things of interest. Sadly, most people easily see this in the non-human parts of nature but seldom transfer that understanding to human societies. The world would be less beautiful if there were only one kind of flower, fish, mammal, or tree. Diversity of species is one of the things that keeps ecosystems strong, healthy, and vital. We know now, for example, that mono-cropping is unhealthy for the plants and animals.

The life of judgment is like the sterile lawn that grows only one type of grass. It causes great harm to the many other types of plants, bugs, and animals that could naturally inhabit that plot of land. The life of self-aware curiosity is like a great forest, full of thousands of species of creatures, all working and living together to create a splendid healthy environment.

Another way to cultivate curiosity and decrease judgment is the practice of *noticing*. When I teach in spiritual direction programs, training students to notice instead of judge is one of the most important aspects of the work. Of course, we begin with noticing ourselves! *How am I feeling? What am I thinking? What do I think about this program?* Often people I work with in spiritual direction or counseling will tell me that they "don't know" what they are thinking and feeling until I ask a few clarifying questions. Then they find the words to describe their internal states with a fair degree of accuracy. It's not that we don't know things; it's that our judging mind prevents us from admitting or acknowledging what we know. People might say they feel guilty for thinking something, or that it's selfish, or not good. The cascade of judgments is endless. Yet as we allow ourselves to notice who we are and who others are, we allow for the possibility of social transformation.

To become self-aware and grounded in a non-judgmental stance in relation to the world is to approach life with tremendous clarity and power. When our spiritual eyes are open, we can see ourselves. When we can hear ourselves, we can hear others. This self-awareness is foundational for a new community where all are valued as beloved of God, full of wonder and promise and the good image of the Divine that appears with such stunning diversity in creation.

This leads directly to the relationship practice for the next chapter, that of powerful presence.

5

ON BECOMING SALT AND LIGHT
The Practice of Powerful Presence

You are the salt of the earth, but if salt has lost its taste, how can its saltiness be restored? It is no longer good for anything but is thrown out and trampled under foot.

You are the light of the world. A city built on a hill cannot be hid. People do not light a lamp and put it under the bushel basket; rather, they put it on the lampstand, and it gives light to all in the house. In the same way, let your light shine before others, so that they may see your good works and give glory to your Father in heaven.

—Matthew 5:13-16

What Do I Say?

Several years ago, one of my best friends contracted a fatal lung disease because agricultural chemicals were stored next to the bedroom he had as a child. I went to visit him for a few days shortly before he died. By that point his lung capacity was so compromised that he could barely walk down his hallway to the living room even on maximum oxygen, so we spent the time just sitting and talking when he was able.

On the second day of the visit, Wren said, "It's so wonderful that you are here doing this and that you are able to just sit with me while I die." I thanked him but suggested that this wasn't a particularly fantastic thing to do. He disagreed and told me that everyone slowly disappeared as his disease progressed. When he first got sick and there was hope that there might be a cure or something to keep the illness at bay for a while, lots of people showed up, mostly to do things. However, as it became clear that he was dying and that there was nothing to "do," friends came by less. People were busy, and there were a lot of reasons not to come.

As a pastor, I have heard and seen this story many times. Friends and family of someone who is dying or severely ill stay away because they do not know how to cope with suffering that cannot be relieved by some action. They don't know what to do or say or if it's okay to be sad, and this points us toward our next vital relationship practice: powerful presence.

Within the bounded environment where we are doing our community practices to manifest the blessed community, where we are becoming more self-aware and curious and not judging people who are different from us, we are also confronted with our own limitations and the reality that suffering and death are non-negotiable parts of the material world.

In our society, a great deal of activity is dedicated to avoiding suffering and death. Anti-aging supplements, plastic surgery, exercise to keep you young, and marketing that tells us that "sixty is the new forty" perpetuate the illusion that we can somehow cheat death. Paradoxically, this illusion causes more suffering than it avoids. Whenever we recognize, consciously or subconsciously, that we cannot prevent suffering, we marginalize those whose presence would force us to look at the reality of death. In a transformed society, we let go of this frenetic activity and allow ourselves to be present to *all* aspects of life in the material world. Powerful presence is a relational practice that creates space for God's love, action, and direction in ourselves and our communities.

Another Problematic Passage

In the passage for this chapter, Jesus points to salt and light as two small things that create large positive effects. As we shall see, this is exactly what the practice of powerful presence does both individually and in social systems. However, before we get to that understanding of Jesus' words, we once again need to address the ways this passage has been used as a tool of oppression, because that is how most Christians have heard it taught and preached.

As with many of Jesus' words, these sound one way when they are viewed from the perspective of the powerful and quite another when they are viewed by the marginalized and oppressed. The "city on the hill" image, as well as the general assertion that Christianity is the correct religion and the religion of the "civilized," has been used for generations by conquering empires as a means of justifying Christian supremacy and oppression of all kinds. The Doctrine of Discovery, a series of Papal Bulls written in the mid-fifteenth century, gave religious justification for conquest of the non-European world by Christian rulers. In the USA, the current rise of Christian Nationalism is the latest version of this tendency. If I see myself as the just conqueror who has all the best ideas, the best civilization, and God on my side, I can justify all manner of evil in the name of my greatness. Every nation that is founded on some notion of supremacy or superiority, whether it is explicitly theocratic or not, is founded on the concept that its religion is the best and that all should bow down to the ruler who lives in the city on the hill.

But Jesus wasn't talking to the rich and the powerful, so this passage cannot be about them nor should it be used to justify their actions. Rather, Jesus is speaking to the very people the Roman Empire was oppressing. To those living in a military occupation zone, the idea that they, rather than a Roman senator or even a Roman citizen, would be a positive presence in the world, not to mention the bearers of God's light, was unimaginable. Anyone who's ever had an honest conversation with someone from a marginalized group knows full well what sort of messages are given to people in that position. Even within the majority group in a conventional society, the slope of the pyramid of success is steep, and most slide to the bottom of the heap. Anyone who occupies either of these social locations, the marginalized or those who are labeled "unsuccessful," experiences a constant drumbeat of negativity about their worth as human beings and their value to society.

Within the circles of those seeking positive social transformation, there is currently significant conversation about centering the voices of the oppressed and the marginalized. The logic behind this is simple. First, it recognizes and reinforces the humanity of those whose humanity is so often denied. Second, centering these voices elevates the point of view of people whose understanding about the nature of society and oppression is rarely heard. As those in power develop the self-awareness to understand their privileged social location, they remove themselves as obstacles to full inclusion and justice. This requires that those on the margins move into the contour of any conversation related to social transformation. This centering behavior is exactly what Jesus was teaching two thousand years ago. The poor and those laboring under military occupation are the light of the world. Those who could never live in or afford even a house are the ones who live in the hilltop city.

Just as with the Beatitudes, this passage is an inversion of the norms of the societies of the world. Those who engage in social transformation actively embrace this inversion and encourage one another in practices that move us collectively toward a different ordering of society. With this view of our passage, we can develop an understanding of how presence is an essential practice in the journey of transformation.

Understanding Spiritual Spaciousness

I'm old enough to have watched *Star Trek* from its start as a television series. Sitting close to a tiny black and white TV, we looked forward to the great opening music and the stirring proclamation that space is the final frontier. As a student of the spiritual life, I have found those words oddly prophetic. From the perspective of the life of contemplation, the space in us and between us is indeed an unknown frontier.

When I talk about spiritual space, I find that most people have little idea what I'm trying to describe. This isn't too surprising, given our culture. Once the first factory was built at the dawn of the Industrial Revolution, company owners realized that the best way to make money was to have that factory running all the time. This was the beginning of a relentless march to fill all the space in our lives.

We've discussed how we fill our time, but we also fill our physical space. We clutter our rooms, our houses, and our rented storage units. As factories around the world continue to churn out products, we fill the oceans, beaches, and landfills; soon there will be no space on earth that isn't full of something we've made. The Great Pacific garbage patch in the Pacific Ocean is currently twice the size of Texas and rapidly growing.

This physical clutter goes along with mental clutter. Our mind is full of thoughts and feelings: to-do lists, worries, shoulds, and judgments. Every corner of our being is full. This even happens at so-called "retreats" where every waking minute of the program is full of a talk, a group, another lecture, or a worship service full of words. Space now scares us.

The effect of this clutter is to crowd God out of our experience and our lives. One of the great confusions regarding spiritual teachings and the spiritual life is the issue of God's presence. When we discuss the practice of prayer and the process of connecting to God, it can sound like we are making God appear, as if God wasn't there or was hiding. At this point in the discussion, someone inevitably says, "God is everywhere and always present. We don't make God appear, so I don't have to do anything to have God be near me." This assertion is technically correct but reveals a misunderstanding of space.

As three-dimensional material beings, when we fill the space we occupy with distractions, God is crowded out. It's not that God isn't there, it's that God is patient and gracious and doesn't tend to intrude upon our lives. If we choose to fill our minds with things that are a distraction from God, God kindly steps aside. Conversely, if we allow space in our hearts, minds, calendars, and relationships, then God appears almost magically. A long-standing joke among colleagues and friends with whom I run retreats is, "We didn't do much, and God showed up again." You provide the space and the tools to pay attention, and the Spirit shows up.

However, the openness is uncomfortable for those who are not used to allowing space. One manifestation of this discomfort is the frequently heard comment, "I don't like silence." While silence and spaciousness are not the same, silence is a tool to help us inhabit spiritual space. Our discomfort is a manifestation of the truth that space is like a frontier that is unknown, vast, and full of things we do not understand and do not have control over.

We fill the space in our lives to attempt to control ourselves and our environment. From a social point of view, this is one of the most problematic aspects of our relationship with space. When the natural human desire to control ourselves and our environment is projected outward into a social space, those with power fill that space with social rules and norms that benefit them.

Anyone who has been paying attention to justice movements in the USA is familiar with the phrase, "[doing some activity] while Black." This phrase is applied to a common, legal, nonthreatening activity a Black person was doing before that person was arrested, harassed, or killed. Thus, you have "driving while Black," "shopping while Black," "grilling while Black." The tragic reality behind these phrases is that Black people in America are not allowed to inhabit social spaces in the same way White people are. This is an example of the control of social space. Another common example is of White men dominating conversations whether they know what they are talking about or not. Again, the rules of society dictate that these particular people are given priority, and they learn to take that space without any thought or consideration of their social position.

When we practice relaxing into space, allowing ourselves to be in space rather than trying to fill the space, we disrupt our social and individual rules, and we experience this disruption as discomfort. However, as we continue in our practice, this discomfort begins to disappear and is replaced by an experience of God's presence because, remember, God was there all the time.

The practice of powerful presence is therefore not just about showing up for someone or something. This is valuable, but powerful presence as a spiritual practice, especially regarding social transformation, is much more than an individual effort. As we inhabit and become empty space, we allow the spiritual reality that has always been there to emerge in a powerful way. This brings us back to the salt and light metaphors. Both salt and light are facilitators. Salt allows us to notice the other tastes in the food we are eating, and light allows us to see objects around us.

Powerful presence is the practice of creating an empty space so that God's Spirit may be noticed in the crowded human space that is generally full of clutter and distraction. In such an open setting, the Spirit has room to move and work, and suddenly an environment that felt ordinary or stuck or devoid of life begins to transform. This explains why great social movements are often accelerated by the small actions of a single person, even as these movements are of course the result of many people acting over long periods of time. People such as Greta Thunberg sitting outside the Swedish parliament or Rosa Parks sitting on a bus are vehicles for the spirit of justice that can emerge when given room to flow. This understanding of space also helps explain the paradoxical observation of the spiritual life that "doing nothing" regularly results in a tremendous amount of positive action in the world. Our spacious presence, the act of non-action, allows for the powerful action of God in the world.

Practicing Presence

The practice of powerful presence for social transformation can be broken down into a few steps we repeat throughout our lives: recognizing the value of presence over product; letting go of the need to fix; relaxing into space; allowing, creating, and taking space for those who have been actively deprived of space by the dominant culture.

The way these steps will appear and manifest in a community seeking the transformation of the Spirit will vary depending on the social location of the practitioners. Presence is a wonderful example of this rarely discussed truth. Those of the dominant culture are used to taking up space, while those who have been oppressed have been trained to hold back and remain on the margins. Thus, in the salt and light world of Jesus, the first group practices presence by taking up less space, while the second group takes up more space. These aren't different practices, but rather they are the same practice of powerful presence applied within a social setting.

As mentioned before, our current industrialized, corporatized society values product and production above all else. "Likes," "hits," "sales," "followers," and ultimately "profit" are the most important and most highly remunerated measures.

Therefore, it is a radical and countercultural act to recognize that the spiritual life places far more value on presence than product. Retraining our thinking and the thinking of our community in this way is a profound spiritual practice that requires effort. We must consciously bring our attention to the value of spiritual connection to be present.

This first step confronts us with the fact that the quintessential product of the helping professions is the need to fix. Remember the story of my friend Wren. As people realized they couldn't fix his illness, they stopped coming to visit him. When we are confronted with our limited ability to fix almost anything, our social conditioning kicks in and we feel inadequate, helpless, and guilt-ridden.

Yet presence isn't about fixing; it's about being there. In humility and with self-awareness, I recognize my limitations, but I do not shrink back. I allow myself to inhabit the space as both a being made in the image of God and as a conduit for the Spirit of love, light, salt. I do not need to fix everything, but I can be present anywhere. So, we can relax and attend to our environment in a loving way. This brings a power and a healing to any situation, even one where someone is dying.

This act of relinquishing the need to fix points to another essential aspect of the practice of powerful presence: We can tolerate being in the presence of the suffering of the world, even as we cannot make it go away. Those who are suffering long for loving presence, yet those who need to fix or who are fixated upon their production value do not have either the time or the inclination to be present to the suffering of the world. This is why there are so many social tropes and concepts that blame those who suffer for their plight, as I mentioned earlier, using the example of the poor being perceived as lazy. Spirituality circles regularly fall into the trap of telling those who suffer that they don't have enough faith or didn't do the correct thing to attract good energy. If we can pretend that those who suffer do so by choice, we can dismiss their suffering.

But the behavior Jesus calls for in the Sermon on the Mount draws us into the suffering of the world so that it may be healed. The empire hides the truth that most of the worst suffering on the planet is caused by the empire and its war, greed, and violence. The practices that draw us to the beloved community also draw us into the suffering of the world so we can see the suffering clearly and then participate with God in the world's transformation.

These first steps lead to the ability to relax into the space we all inhabit. Our spiritual practices increase our awareness of our three-dimensionality and our embodiment in a material world. We become more curious about our spaciousness. We learn to tolerate silence as we recognize that the space we inhabit is teeming with divine life and energy. Such awareness draws us lovingly into the space as we recognize the value of our being.

Anyone who has ever spent time with a baby knows a great deal about the practice of powerful presence. When we are with a baby, we immediately recognize the value of this tiny creature. I am a new grandfather, and no one needs to give me a talk on the value of my grandson. Yet the capitalist empire considers him worthless except as an object to use to sell baby products to: He doesn't produce valuable products; he mostly just crawls around making a mess; he's unproductive and ineffective. Yet sharing space with him is an activity of limitless value that is the result of his existence. This is presence, and it's something that we understand. It's also something that is socialized out of us in school and work.

When we inhabit social space in a loving and peaceful way, our desire for the manifestation of justice and the kingdom of God in these spaces grows. This means that our practice of powerful presence allows our behavior to reflect the ordering of that kingdom. This is one of the concrete ways our practice reveals the inversion of the empire. As we become aware of our social location, we show up in the space in new ways. If we are part of the dominant culture, we become content to be present and take a step back. If we are part of the groups who have been oppressed, we are empowered to be present with more life and energy. The sum of this activity on a social level is that indeed all are salt and light, and in our transformed relationships, all are seen as fully human. As our humanity is revealed by presence, we are led directly to our next relational practice, compassionate relationship.

6

ON OATHS AND CARING
The Practice of Compassionate Relationship

Again, you have heard that it was said to those of ancient times, "You shall not swear falsely, but carry out the vows you have made to the Lord." But I say to you: Do not swear at all, either by heaven, for it is the throne of God, or by the earth, for it is his footstool, or by Jerusalem, for it is the city of the great King. And do not swear by your head, for you cannot make one hair white or black. Let your word be "Yes, Yes" or "No, No"; anything more than this comes from the evil one.

—Matthew 5:33-37

Why Oaths?

The taking and making of oaths is a practice common to every human society. We take oaths in court, people who become citizens take oaths, and contracts are a form of oath taking. Given the ubiquity of oaths, it's not a surprise that Jesus mentions them. What is unusual is how he talks about them, so let us see how he is turning a commonplace activity into a prayer practice for social transformation.

An oath is a promise that is supported by reference to some greater power. People developed oaths for the simple reason that human beings lie and don't do what they say they are going to do. So, whenever we make a promise, the issue of enforcement arises. *What if I don't keep my promise? Who is going to hold me to it?* This issue appears in the Hebrew scripture because promises and the making or breaking of them is an issue of justice, and the Bible tells us again and again that God is interested in justice. One of the hallmarks of the kingdom of God is justice.

Oath-taking is preemptively submitting to the decision of a court that will find us guilty if we do not keep our oath. If I swear to God, I expect God to hold me to account for breaking my promise. The unstated assumption here is that the fear of God is a deterrent to breaking an oath. And perhaps for some it is.

However, we must admit that God does not show up out of the sky to enforce oaths. We know that people break their promises all the time, large and small, and that holding people accountable to their promises is difficult if not impossible. This explains why there are so many threats of violence associated with oaths and promises. I grew up under the international doctrine of MAD—mutually assured destruction—which is the frankly horrific idea that the treaties between the US and Russia signed during the Cold War were backed by so many nuclear weapons that the entire planet could be destroyed. Apparently, pinky swearing to God wouldn't have been enough to secure world peace, and of course no one would have even considered swearing to God as a way to solve the Cold War.

Jesus understands that far too often oath-taking is the opposite of what it appears to be. Rather than being a way of enforcing promises, it is a way of hiding our intention to default on our promises. If I swear on something or someone who I know will not help enforce my oath, either because it is an invisible deity, a dead relative, or an idea, then I can appear to be genuine but know that no one will come to harm me if I renege on the promise sealed by the oath.

In the modern era, we can see this deception at work as contracts become longer and longer, filled with more clauses that try to cover every possible contingency, every instance in which one of the parties might try and break the contract. We now take three-hundred-page oaths, and still people fail to deliver. This is the problem Jesus is addressing, and the solution he proposes is the spiritual practice of compassionate relationship.

The Corrosive Nature of Inauthentic Relationship

Saying yes and saying no sounds so easy, but it is not. Yet again we find that simple practices are hard. The depth of this practice can be understood only if we continue to examine the nature of relationships within the kingdoms of the earth.

A few years ago, I began watching the TV show *Atypical*. I don't remember why I started watching, but I found it revolutionary both personally and professionally, as it introduced me to the current discussion related to neuroatypia.[11] Even if you are not familiar with this term or these issues, you have most certainly heard of autism or people "on the spectrum." While this field is vast and complex, here I wish to draw attention to some of the relational aspects found in the conversations about neurotypical versus neuroatypical people. Personally, I have known since childhood that something was "wrong" about the way I engage in social relationships. I was always missing social cues or saying the wrong thing, but I could never put my finger on what exactly was happening. No matter how many times I asked people, I could never get a clear answer. Then I discovered the world of neurodiversity.

While it isn't fully understood by any means, we are coming to realize that there are people who do not display all the symptoms of autism or other neuroatypical conditions, yet they do have neurological functioning different from the dominant culture, particularly in social situations. I mention this because one of the most significant differences between the neuroatypical world and that of neurotypical people is the issue of lying or authenticity. One of my most significant areas of social confusion was that I could never understand why people around me often lied. Such behavior literally makes my brain hurt, yet it happens all the time.

To give you an idea of what this looks like from the perspective of neuroatypia, here is a partial list of imagined rules of a society run according to how neuroatypical brains work:

- Don't stare into people's eyes when you're talking. It's rude and makes people feel like you're staring into their soul, which is creepily intimate.
- Say what you mean to say. It's rude to drop hints or dance around a topic expecting others to read your mind.
- Avoid meaningless small talk. It's rude to the person who has to listen to you ramble on about the weather when they have better things to do.
- Don't ask people how they are doing if you only want to hear a positive answer. When someone replies telling you how not okay they are, it's rude to judge them for honestly answering your question.
- It's rude to ask for someone's feedback and then treat them like they did something wrong when they give you their honest opinion.
- Avoid changing plans last minute. It's rude to the person who spent their entire day mentally preparing themselves for the event.[12]

If you examine the items on this list, which is meant to give neurotypical people a perspective on their own behavior, you can see how one of the hallmarks of "normal" society is an emphasis on being inauthentic. The effect this has on people and society is significant and highly corrosive. As we grow, we learn that we cannot really trust what people are saying or doing. The habit of digital ghosting—ceasing all digital communication—is another example of this problem. Because this practice is so common, when someone is talking to me, telling me that they want to do something or they are going to get back to me about an idea or a project, I have learned that I can never be sure if what they are saying means anything or is true.

My point here is not to say that people who are neuroatypical are more spiritual or that neuroatypia is a manifestation of the kingdom of God (although some have made this assertion, even claiming that Jesus was neuroatypical[13]). Rather, this is simply another lens through which we can see the dominant culture and the kingdoms of the world. It offers us another perspective.

Looking at neurotypical patterns of communication from a spiritual point of view, from the point of view of a God who declares that God is "the truth," we can understand how endless tiny betrayals undermine the formation of the beloved community. How can I believe that you love me if you are constantly telling me lies?

And this particular type of lying is part of the social fabric of the kingdoms of the world; a reality currently encapsulated by the term *gaslighting*, derived from the 1944 movie

Gaslight, in which a man drives his wife insane by lying to her about the gaslights in their house. Gaslighting happens whenever someone is told that something that is obviously true is false. Social examples of this are White people who deny the racism of our society in the face of obvious examples of racism, corporate executives who deny that their companies are polluting the environment even as the environment becomes more polluted, and parents or partners who deny their abusive behavior even as those who are abused experience the effects of such abuse. These are all ways the powerful attempt to maintain their position by denying the oppressive actions that prevent justice and the formation of the kingdom of God.

Practicing Compassion

The antidote to inauthentic relationship is the spiritual practice of compassionate relationship. These are popular terms, so I need to define what they mean from the perspective of the spiritual tradition. How do we get to yes and no?

People I work with in counseling and spiritual direction often start to wonder if everyone is a narcissist. To some degree, the answer is yes. While there is a clinical psychological definition of narcissism that doesn't apply to everyone, the basic ego process places us—ourselves and our identity—at the center of our universe, a process that is inherently narcissistic. This is why the practice of self-awareness in chapter 4 is so hard and so important. We must practice getting outside of ourselves and our own little view of the world.

This narcissism limits our ability to see another person and their world, which also limits how much we care about another person or how our actions affect others. Relational dynamics and our descriptions of them are complex and tricky. For example, codependence, the process whereby we support another person's toxic habits, can be described in ways similar to compassion when we say, "I just wanted to help" or "I didn't want to hurt their feelings." Kindness, or the mask of kindness, is often used to describe and support inauthentic relationships.

Compassionate relationship as a spiritual practice is quite different from fake niceness. Compassion is an experience that begins with self-compassion. In our spiritual life and practice, we begin to see ourselves as we truly are, messy human beings. Once I saw a cute romantic comedy about a young couple trying to get together. It was a fairly standard film; however, I was shocked by a series of scenes in which the woman tried not to go to the bathroom at the man's apartment. Apparently, trying to not admit certain bodily functions early in dating is a real issue that women must deal with.[14] This struck me as so sad and yet understandable given our level of inauthenticity in relationships.

Our spiritual life allows us to fully embrace our humanity—our failings, successes, health, illnesses—and this loving embrace creates in us a warm and deep caring for who we are as people. Yet this caring doesn't then stay with us. For thousands of years, spiritual practitioners have recognized that true loving-kindness is the antidote to narcissism. When we experience this deep caring, it naturally spreads out from our heart to the world. Now I clearly see how everyone else I meet is also a frail and messy human being.

From this new point of view, we then ask ourselves how we would like to be treated. The answer, naturally, is with love and care. This conclusion is inescapable and leads to a deep desire for the practice of compassionate relationship.

Creating a Space for Compassionate Relationship

It's so easy to say that Jesus wants us to be compassionate and have authentic relationships. Yet we know that these are incredibly difficult spiritual teachings. Consider all the internal and external rules that imprison us in a fake world. The things we are afraid to say, the criticism and ostracism we face if we tell the truth, and the traps we set for one another as we ask for comments and feedback and then ghost those who give us answers we find insulting. It goes on and on.

This is why spiritual communities have always tried to create safe spaces for the practice of compassionate relationship. We need intentional spaces in which we can practice something different from how we were formed by the world. In the Christian monastic tradition, the vow that we will not run away, is integral to such a space. Our practice of compassionate relationship generates awareness that we make mistakes; we fail, and we do and say things that are misunderstood or are unhelpful or even hurtful. Usually, these behaviors are quite unintentional. So, it is only within an environment of forgiveness, expanding self-awareness, and commitment to a loving community that we can become compassionate and authentic.

Many people, particularly those who are oppressed by the kingdoms of the world, have almost no space to practice compassion or authenticity; frankly, their lives are too dangerous. If we are talking about serious social transformation, it is incumbent upon all of us to foster whatever small spaces we can where some compassion can be practiced. Here are a few questions, tips and pointers that can guide your practice.

Begin with your own sense of compassion and authenticity. Do you hold yourself with loving-kindness? Are you forgiving and honest with yourself? If you consider yourself a caring person, does that caring extend to you? Do you practice seeing yourself, your life, and your activities honestly and compassionately? For example, I often hear people critique themselves and their activities while they list all the things they do and are responsible for; this is a concrete demonstration of a lack of self-compassion and a lack of authentic honesty.

Now begin to look at your social spaces such as work, church, clubs, family, and networks of relationships either in person or online. What do you notice about the stated and unstated rules in these spaces? Are there clearly things that are allowed and not allowed? How do you feel about these rules? How do you see and experience the other people in these social structures? Does your compassion extend to them? Who are you least able to see in a compassionate light, and what does this tell you about yourself?

As you consider these systems of relationships and bring your awareness to how they are formed, what desires do you notice arising? Could these systems change to make them safer and more authentic? Have you grown beyond these systems? Are you perhaps seeking new systems that are more interested in compassionate practice? What is keeping you from moving toward these new places?

One very simple yet powerful question I often assign people who are working on compassionate relationship is, "What do you want?" I encourage people to ask this of themselves not just for large things like their careers, but for everyday small things: *What do you want to eat? What do you want to do this afternoon?* The fact that is such a hard question for so many of us gets to the heart of what Jesus is talking about in this passage on oaths. The oaths we've all taken, mostly without knowing, are oaths to dishonest habits and patterns of behavior.

The practice of "yes and no" is the practice of acknowledging our authentic desires as they arise out of compassion for ourselves and others. As we let go of our imperial oaths and are honest with ourselves, we find that we do, in fact, know what we want. And then we can begin to move into the world from the new space of caring, compassionate relationship—movement that creates social transformation.

"Mindfulness of speech" is another way to describe this practice of "yes and no." To be spiritually mindful of our speech is to speak from a place of compassionate relationship. So often when people say, "I'll call you," it's simply a mindless habit. We say what we were taught was "nice" or what we hope might happen, or we want to not hurt the person. However, when we bring our awareness to what we say, we utter only those things that are true, those things we authentically wish to say. This practice creates a relational space that is truly loving and real and allows for the flourishing of the beloved community.

Self-awareness, powerful presence, and compassionate relationship are three spiritual practices that together allow for the possibility of a relational dynamic that is fundamentally different from that of the normal worldly kingdom. Jesus is asking us to practice this new way of being together to promote a loving social reality and create a new way of relating to material goods and sustenance. These are the subject of the next three chapters as we listen for how Jesus describes the material life of the kingdom of God.

As we come to the end of this section, pause and visualize the relationships in your life. How might these practices change them? How does that feel to you? Is it scary? Liberating? Overwhelming? Exciting? This is the path toward the kin-dom of God.

7

LET'S TALK ABOUT MONEY
The Practice of Serving God

> *No one can serve two masters, for a slave will either hate the one and love the other or be devoted to the one and despise the other. You cannot serve God and wealth.*
>
> —Matthew 6:24

Attending to Material Reality

The practices in the first six chapters set the table for the banquet of the new kingdom. We have prepared the environment and have described how the relationships among those who inhabit that environment are made new. But then what? We do not sit still like statues in the garden; our life on earth is full of action as we live as creatures in the material world. Surely this spiritual life of beloved community must attend to the materiality of our existence. A great failing of spiritual teachings is that they are frequently disconnected from material reality.

The Bible has hundreds of references to material justice, caring for the poor, protecting widows and orphans, and standing up for those who are oppressed and do not have enough to eat or a place to live. But the Bible's intense focus on our economic life is regularly ignored in our church communities, especially those populated by the dominant culture and class. I remember well the terrified looks when I suggested, in a discussion about my salary as pastor, that we post in the church the salaries and economic positions of all our church members! (We didn't do that.) Yet without engaging the economic realities of our life in the world, our spiritualizing never results in social transformation.

These next three chapters discuss practices that focus directly on our material existence. Once we have created the environmental conditions for the kingdom of God, how do we use our "stuff" so that the kingdom can appear? This is one of the central questions Jesus addresses in the Sermon on the Mount, and it is also one of most important questions contemplative communities have addressed throughout history. While people love to quote the monastics' "spiritual teachings," monasticism is an economic system at least as much as a spiritual teaching system. In other words, monasticism sees our economic relationships as inseparable from spiritual teaching. This chapter will discuss the spiritual practice of serving God in connection to wealth, and the next two chapters will take on the practices of radical trust and letting go.

You've Got to Serve Somebody

The Bible passage for this chapter is another famous and familiar line. It has been discussed in thousands of sermons and theological reflections. In Bob Dylan's Christian phase, he turned it into a Grammy-winning message with his song, "Gotta Serve Somebody." Yet the American Christian landscape shows little evidence that all this conversation has produced economic or social transformation. So, what practice is Jesus calling us to in relation to God and money?

Jesus focuses on service as key to this discussion, so we need to spend some time looking at this issue. Many people, especially those of us in wealthy, highly individualistic, societies, do not think of themselves as servants. The felt but possibly unstated response to Jesus' warning that you can't serve two masters is, "I don't serve *any* masters." Many people see "service" as either something from a movie about some royal family in which the servants are constantly running about like so many barely visible rabbits, or something that we might do on a mission trip or some other optional ministry activity. We do not tend to see "service" as fundamental to our human condition. Yet the spiritual traditions assert that we indeed are servants to many things.

Being a servant implies that a person is bound to perform duties or activities for someone or something other than themself. Of course throughout history, servitude and slavery have been negative and abusive experiences. In America, and this is paradoxical in a country that had slaves and then sharecroppers for hundreds of years, the desire to be "free" above all else is deeply imbedded in the mythical culture of the nation. Yet the basic fact of material creature-hood and the ego process of the human mind dictate that being "in service" is a fundamental aspect of our reality. To maintain our existence, we are in service to our bodily functions, hungers, breath, and physical needs. We also are in service to our ego's habitual patterns and our emotional states. When our behavior is so regular and compulsive, we "serve" these habits.

Perhaps you find this description of service as a subconscious activity unfamiliar or even jarring, but creating new paths of awareness in our mind is an essential part of the spiritual life. As created material beings, we spend our lives in service to the things that keep us alive. We are in service to the cycle of the seasons—to the food that is planted in the spring and harvested in the fall—and to the systems our society has created to distribute food. Jesus sees this truth and recognizes that we are in service to whatever provides for our existence. He also recognizes that we become attached to whatever *we believe* provides us with life.

In human society, money and God are two basic sources of nourishment. One is seen and one is unseen. We are told that God provides for all, but in our day-to-day experience, no money means no food. In the ancient world, where most people were subsistence farmers, a failed crop meant no seed for next year's planting, which in turn meant that your family became debt servants, literally servants of money. In the modern world, children learn young that they need to get a job as adults. Modern cities are now full of people who are unhoused because they have, for one reason or another, failed at this basic requirement of our culture. They have become object lessons of the consequences of being judged a poor servant by society.

In these ways, the kingdoms of the world grab our attention and bind us to the world of wealth. It is a bond so strong that we avoid conversations about our economic relationships, even in church communities. We are indeed good and faithful servants of money. But the kingdom of God needs a different kind of service.

Recognizing Our Attachments

Spiritual practice leads us through three stages of recognition or awareness. The first stage is often the most painful. It is the awareness of how things are, the awareness of ourselves and our situation. In the second stage, we become aware of the space beyond the familiar, the space of the unknown. In the third stage, we become aware of God's presence and the wider reality of a world beyond our habitual patterns. The rhythm of practice will cycle us through these stages throughout our lives.

The reason this three-stage journey is necessary at all is that our ego doesn't want us to see our situation clearly. The problem is particularly acute when it comes to money and who we serve. Any talk of money and Jesus will immediately elicit dismissive comments about how unrealistic his teachings were. Pastors who try to preach on economic justice encounter put-downs such as, "It must be nice to get paid to pray." These reactions reflect our collective bond to wealth; we are indeed faithful servants.

Thus, if we are to have a new relationship with material goods, we must commit to the practice of becoming aware of our servitude. This requires courage and self-compassion to make progress in our spiritual journey. While our attachment to money is perhaps embarrassing or difficult to acknowledge, our self-compassion helps us understand that we are simply doing what we have been trained to do by our society.

Our entire commercial economy relies on convincing us that we do not have enough and need to buy more, which of course requires more money. The "keeping up with the Joneses" phenomenon means that we feel the need to purchase the bigger and better toy of the day to maintain our social status, with no regard for any actual need. It is common to see riding mowers large enough for a ten-acre field mowing the tiny lawns of massive suburban houses.

Then there is the "saving for retirement" race. Getting a good job isn't enough because you won't have that job forever. You must save, and you are probably not saving enough. As the retirement investment business will tell you, whether you ask them or not, you need to put away many times your current income to make it through retirement. Just as buying a lawnmower isn't the end of status anxiety, getting a job isn't the end of monetary anxiety. Without millions in the bank, you will find yourself rotting in some horrible nursing home alone and poorly cared for.

These messages that are repeated every day in many different forms are powerful and formative. We should not be surprised or ashamed that they have turned us into servants of wealth; we didn't have another option. This isn't any different from all other habits and habitual patterns, but sometimes issues of money can feel more acute or real because they are so clearly connected to survival. This is a reason we shy away from the critical conversations about material goods when we discuss spirituality. Talking about taking a few minutes a week to do a spiritual practice feels safer and easier than discussing our bank accounts.

Attending to our material attachments is the practice of recognizing these truths regarding wealth. In no way are we dismissing the need for money and care. We are instead allowing ourselves to see all the ways we serve money. Because to serve wealth means that we fully participate in the social systems that give much to some and little to others. It means that we do not serve God.

The Kingdom of Enough

The yearly fights over the federal budget in the US make it crystal clear that there is always enough money for war, but care for people is too expensive. No matter how large the federal deficit becomes, massive new spending is always available to fund wars. Yet spending on healthcare, housing, or education is irresponsible and reckless because we are living beyond our means.

This phenomenon is directly connected to the issue of wealth and service because to serve wealth also means to serve the kingdoms of the world whose primary focus is survival, expansion, and self-preservation. This is why the service of wealth creates the inequalities and injustices that Jesus is trying to address as he encourages us to work toward the kingdom of God. If the service of wealth didn't create social problems, it also would not be a problem. Money in and of itself isn't the issue; it is simply a tool of exchange so the goods people need might be distributed within society. The problem is our *attachments*, our service to *wealth*. Our attachments create the clinging that supports systems that benefit some at the expense of others.

War is the final manifestation of this service of wealth as it is the way societies control others and protect themselves. But the violence of wealth also shows itself in laws that exclude, divide, and oppress. In the end, all these systems serve wealth.

In contrast, the kingdom of God is the kingdom of enough. It shouldn't be a surprise that there is enough food, water, and shelter for everyone on the planet. In the United States alone, there are enough unoccupied houses—second, third, or vacation homes—to give every unhoused person on our streets multiple homes.[15] And we are still arguing about whether it is a good idea or a wasteful handout to make sure children get lunch at school whether they can pay or not, even though approximately a third of the food produced in the United States goes to waste.[16]

People do not have enough despite there being enough, because we serve wealth and not God. Thus, as we consider shifting our service to God, we start by noticing our attachment to money and begin to pay attention to the reality of enough. As with all the practices in this book, this activity is meant to be done collectively. If we are talking about the practice of social transformation, we aren't just talking about saving a bit of money on our clothing bill. We are talking about collective action that can allow us to become part of communities that share and live the reality of abundance.

For more than 1,700 years, the Christian monastic tradition has practiced the reality of abundance through the collective vow of poverty. This vow is generally misunderstood because our service to wealth blinds us to the possibility of service to God. The monastic vow of poverty is not a vow of destitution—that is how the kingdoms of the world often define poverty. The Bible is clear that God wants everyone to have enough to eat and the necessities of life; this is the biblical standard of caring for the widows and orphans. Again, enough money is fine; serving money—serving *wealth*—is the problem.

The monastic vow of poverty is a vow to be content with enough, to have one's basic needs met within the community, and to share all property communally. The members of the community are "poor" in that they do not own things that they can hoard and keep from others. This is the practice of serving God. We rely on God to meet our basic needs through the actions of the community as we do work in the world. Even though this tradition has existed for seventeen centuries, the kingdoms of the world and the servants of wealth continue to claim that such an economic arrangement is unrealistic and impossible.

As we attend to what we serve, we begin to look at our individual and collective economic relationships. We also can consider the following questions about these relationships to help us notice our service relationships. *Do we believe that there is enough in the world? Why do people feel that there isn't enough? How do we relate to the economic resources we have? Do our communities consider economic relationships? How might we begin to practice being in God's service in tangible economic ways?*

These questions can lead to tangible action for economic justice and transformation. As we consider spiritually-driven social transformation, we must ask if we are willing to be inconvenienced by supporting policies that give from the excess of the powerful—those who have too much—to care for those who have been excluded and oppressed.

Reflecting deeply upon these questions helps us become aware of our current relationship to wealth and brings us to the edge of what is new and unknown, that second step of awareness. When we leave the familiar, we encounter anxiety, one of the most powerful forces that keeps the status quo in place. The next teaching from Jesus, and the second practice as we engage the material world for social transformation, directly addresses this important obstacle.

8

FACING ANXIETY
The Practice of Radical Trust

Therefore I tell you, do not worry about your life, what you will eat or what you will drink, or about your body, what you will wear. Is not life more than food and the body more than clothing? Look at the birds of the air: they neither sow nor reap nor gather into barns, and yet your heavenly Father feeds them. Are you not of more value than they? And which of you by worrying can add a single hour to your span of life? And why do you worry about clothing? Consider the lilies of the field, how they grow; they neither toil nor spin, yet I tell you, even Solomon in all his glory was not clothed like one of these. But if God so clothes the grass of the field, which is alive today and tomorrow is thrown into the oven, will he not much more clothe you—you of little faith? Therefore do not worry, saying, "What will we eat?" or "What will we drink?" or "What will we wear?" For it is the gentiles who seek all these things, and indeed your heavenly Father knows that you need all these things. But seek first the kingdom of God and his righteousness, and all these things will be given to you as well.

So do not worry about tomorrow, for tomorrow will bring worries of its own. Today's trouble is enough for today.

—Matthew 6:25-34

Anxiety and the Human Condition

Humans are anxious creatures. Our anxiety arises as we become aware of our mortality, and this is as true now as it was when Jesus walked the earth. Here we have another familiar, clear, and direct passage from Jesus. Once again, people accuse Jesus of being unrealistic and out of touch. It's fine for Jesus to not be anxious; he's God. But for us, living without anxiety seems easy to say and impossible to do.

But Jesus wasn't a fool and knew what he was saying. He was aware of the social and political realities of his time. He was talking to people who faced far more danger and social unrest than most of us do in modern America. So, we need to take him seriously, especially if we are committed to social transformation.

As with some of our previous passages, we must begin with what this passage is *not* saying, with the ways Jesus' teaching has been distorted and abused. Sadly, many Christian people and traditions have focused on the "you of little faith" part to make people feel guilty about their concerns and responsible for their own misfortune. If they can "think positive," then nothing bad will happen to them. Many have been taught to feel that they haven't had enough faith and that is why they have gotten cancer or haven't been able to live the life they desired. But Jesus' teachings on anxiety are not a test or condemnation.

In this passage, Jesus clearly states that we will have troubles. His isn't some prosperity gospel promise where the right amount of faith will bring riches, healing, and happiness. Furthermore, this isn't another promise of heaven. No, Jesus is asking us as a human community to relate to our lives in a way that is different from the usual human response to being alive.

The spiritual teachings of all traditions see that human beings spend most of our mental time and energy in the past and the future but not in the present. As Jesus indicates, we are worried about what the future will bring and about how the past has negatively affected our lives. We worry about our economic future, and we worry if we said the right thing to our friend. *Did I choose the right career? Did I spend enough time with my children? Did I save enough for retirement?*

These thoughts create the anxiety we experience daily. This collective anxiety then leads to an unjust society where those who can amass wealth hoard it for themselves and their families, and those who do not have access to wealth find themselves in ever more dire conditions. This social inequity serves to create more anxiety as it validates the concerns that we all have, which, in turn, creates a more repressive society. It's a vicious downward spiral. We can see the results of this in the United States, which is one of the wealthiest and most anxious countries in the world.

Yet we do not reside in the past and the future. We exist in the present. Again, this is an ancient observation and teaching shared among all spiritual traditions. In many ways, it is a self-evident statement, and the fact that it needs to be taught is in and of itself symptomatic of our anxious state. When we allow anxiety from our thoughts about the past and future into our present, it fills the spiritual space we need to listen for God. When we are consumed with anxiety, we cannot be fully in our bodies; we cannot see and experience life as it is; we are not aware of the life-giving spirit in our midst. Most of the time, people who are experiencing anxiety are, at the moment they are anxious, just fine. However, anxiety is a great cloud that sits on our minds and hearts, obscuring what is right in front of us. Worrying about things that never happen not only costs us years of lost energy and suffering, but we also lose the opportunity to listen to the Spirit and imagine a more just society. This is what Jesus is addressing.

Radical Trust as Material Beings

In the previous chapter, we addressed the issue of where allegiance lies as we live an embodied life. This chapter extends these reflections because anxiety is one of the most powerful emotional processes that keep us in service to wealth and direct our attention away from God. Jesus points to radical trust as he observes the wonder of creation and God's care for every creature. Again, this isn't a naive, romantic teaching that ignores the suffering in the world; it is a powerful observation about the care and love that are built into creation by the presence and power of the Spirit.

Radical trust in God is radical trust in the kingdom of enough. It is an appreciation of God with us. When we live in the present, we live in our embodied selves and therefore we can appreciate creation and the capacity of creation to care for all. Like all the practices in this book, the practice of radical trust is simple but not easy. The kingdoms of the world are invested in making us anxious.

Church communities show that anxiety has a hold even in places that proclaim the wonders and power of God every week. For instance, most churches that die do so with money in the bank, often a lot of money. Rainy day funds were saved up because the community had the same anxieties that rule the rest of the wold. Yet the rain came, the community died, and it never occurred to them to use the money to do something new, help those around them, or seek and trust the guidance of God. No, they did the same thing, saved the money, and when they finally closed their doors, the funds just rolled up the denominational hill to the next bank account where the money is being saved for another rainy day. This is such a common occurrence that the presbytery (a regional body of the Presbyterian Church USA) I served in had an entire fund created from money coming in from churches that were closing. One of the country churches I served had fewer than twenty members but was projected to close with over a quarter of a million dollars on hand.

This shows the challenge of radical trust. It's easy to say that God is with us, but it's far harder to act as if that's true. Even the phrase "rainy day" is an interesting one in this regard. Rain brings life to the earth. Why isn't a "rainy day" a sign of God's presence and care? This new view is the view of radical trust. It is the view that we find when our spiritual life heals us from anxiety, the fog clears, and we begin to see how God is working in our lives and the life of the world.

Anxiety and Community

Even when this passage about anxiety isn't used overtly negatively, it is often still spiritualized and individualized. It becomes simply about my mental health and my anxious thoughts rather than about the community and the kingdom of God. Remember, the idea that Jesus is teaching just about individual spirituality is a lie that prevents us from living into the kingdom of God. In this case, anxiety and social structures are intimately connected. It is perfectly reasonable to be anxious about social safety nets that often do not help people. Further, powerful people see the anxiety caused by an uncaring society and want no part of the danger, so they are unwilling to promote significant change. Therefore, we must consider how the community uses its resources when we consider anxiety and material goods.

The cure to anxiety isn't just an abstract or spiritual trust in God. It requires us to act and act together in concrete ways to transform society so that the abundance of this world reaches everyone. As our spiritual life reduces our anxiety and increases our trust in God, we are called to extend this trust to others and live in the world in new ways.

Several years ago, our ministry (Minnesota Institute of Contemplation and Healing [MICAH]) partnered with our local hospital to create an integrative medicine clinic. This was an unusual type of clinical practice that challenged many of the long-held assumptions about medical care by addressing the body, mind, and spirit. It was successful beyond anyone's expectations. However, not all challenges were welcomed by the hospital. When we began working with the hospital administration to create the staffing plan, we said we wanted to create an equitable salary structure. There would be great parity between the receptionist, doctors, nurses, and the other medical practitioners. Although the hospital was supportive of the clinic in general, they absolutely wouldn't budge on this point. Such an economic arrangement was unthinkable.

This story is an example of the power of context and the power of the kingdoms of the world. The people who were telling us we couldn't distribute funds more equitably were speaking for the principalities and powers of the world that want to keep us anxious and concerned that there isn't enough. On the face of it, our request was benign and harmless: Why should anyone care if everyone makes similar salaries? Yet we can see that it really is a radical and highly destabilizing request. If the word got out that one clinic had equal pay, then maybe everyone would ask for equal pay. If one doctor refused to participate in an economic system that gives too much to some while others barely get paid a living wage, then perhaps other doctors would be asked to give up some of their wages, which of course might lead to them leaving the hospital. The system couldn't tolerate this risk, and yet this is exactly the type of change that social transformation demands. A decrease in overall anxiety arises not by spiritualizing teachings but through concrete action in solidarity with those who are in unsafe spaces and unstable economic conditions.

Practicing Radical Trust

The spiritual practice of radical trust, of becoming less anxious, is about healing from our individual and collective trauma, our disconnection from the divine. To love ourselves, our neighbors, God is to become aligned with a reality that is full of care, life, and what we need. Yet as I've pointed to, we live in a separated reality, anxious about not having or being enough even when there is a great bounty right in front of us.

One specific practice that I frequently recommend is "reality testing." Our anxious minds are constantly lying to us about a world that might exist but rarely does. Many years ago, a friend was entering a graduate program. Every semester there was a lot of anxiety that they would fail, and every semester they got straight As. By the third semester, when the concern about failing still arose, I asked my friend if this concern was at all real. Eventually they had to admit that it wasn't.

Reality testing is an awareness practice that draws our attention to what is happening. When we find ourselves concerned about something, we ask ourselves, *Is my concern real?* This brings our focus toward the truth of our situation, whatever that may be. *Are our fears grounded in reality? Are they likely to come true? Is there anything we can do to assess the validity of our concerns?* These are questions that both individuals and groups can ask. In most cases, our anxiety is baseless. And if it is not, then this practice can help us to address the situation.

Because reality testing brings us into contact with the present, it is indeed a "spiritual" practice. God is in reality, not in the anxious fantasies of our minds. When we come closer to reality, we approach the Spirit moving in the world. Often, this reveals how our community can engage the social transformation that is possible but hidden by our anxieties.

This is what Jesus means by today's worries are enough. Today's worries are real, and because they are real, they are manageable, especially in a community of care. There are countless stories about people who have come together in the face of tragedy to help others through difficulties. And in these stories, there is enough, sometimes more than enough, to take care of the problem. What if we greeted every day as both a day of abundance and a day of tragedies to face in our abundance? It would completely change our society. Are we able to trust God to meet us in real life?

In every community—including churches—it is essential to address the anxieties that hold it back from trusting the Spirit and being an agent of social transformation. I've mentioned the practice of hoarding money, and there are many other ways churches let fear and anxiety blind them to the needs of their communities. On the other hand, churches that reach out in trust and deepen their connection to God find themselves working powerfully for good in the world. This move from anxiety to trust is indeed a spiritual practice. We must be intentional about it and engage practices that draw us into the "todays" of our lives so we can embody our spiritual teachings.

The final chapter in this section on material-world practices addresses letting go, another spiritual practice that opens us to social transformation.

9

ON CLINGING TO TREASURES
The Practice of Letting Go

Do not store up for yourselves treasures on earth, where moth and rust consume and where thieves break in and steal, but store up for yourselves treasures in heaven, where neither moth nor rust consumes and where thieves do not break in and steal. For where your treasure is, there your heart will be also.
—Matthew 6:19-21

Simplicity and Repetition

By this point in the book, it may seem like all these teachings of Jesus are the same or at least point toward similar things. In a sense, that is true. All spiritual teachings move toward the same thing, but they get at it from different perspectives. Spirituality is simple in the sense of orienting us toward the

Divine. As Jesus later says in Matthew, the whole of the Law is summed up by the command to love God and love your neighbor as yourself (see 22:34-40). Pretty simple.

The spiritual life is like the instructions on a shampoo bottle: "Rinse, Lather, Repeat." We come to ourselves and our practice over and over again in the same way with the same intention to pay attention. The problem is us: We forget, we get confused, and we run wildly down the rabbit holes of our minds and get lost. Also, life appears to be extremely complex, so it's reasonable for us to think that we need a new teaching for every situation and every generation. The empires of the world exacerbate this complexity and confusion to control us. Bureaucracies, legal entanglements, social rules, etiquette, the pressures to survive, and the obvious lack of care in so many social spaces all bear down on us, unsettling our peace of mind and our contemplation. So, repetition is vital for the spiritual life because it brings us back again and again, drawing our attention to God and to love.

This chapter is our final teaching and practice related to material goods. In chapter 7, we looked at the orientation of our life and the practice of serving God. In chapter 8, we examined anxiety and the practice of radical trust. And in this chapter, we turn to letting go.

Not About Going to Heaven

"If behaving properly won't get me into heaven, then why the hell should I do it?" This is a real quote. It was said to me angrily by a man who'd gone to church his entire life.

He was distressed because I was talking about the present kingdom of God and not the afterlife. The key point is that this man was a regular church-goer. He'd heard thousands of sermons, gone to Sunday school as a kid, and had been confirmed. I share this story not to denigrate him but to show how prevalent the focus on the afterlife has been in Christian congregations for hundreds of years. He was a product of his formation.

This chapter's scripture passage is another one that has been used to convince people that the only point of Christianity is to get through life with enough good behavior to get to heaven. Storing up treasures in heaven, even though Jesus says nothing here about *going* to heaven, is interpreted by the imperial religion as another teaching about the afterlife. Social transformation and upheaval are to be avoided at all costs. Just as the dog in the movie *Up!* was distracted every time he saw a squirrel, we are distracted from Jesus' true teachings by promises of heaven.

If we look at the retirement savings industry, which I discussed above, as just one example, we can see how such an interpretation leads to social behavior that basically obliterates Jesus' real message. We are told every day in commercials, billboards, or by our financial advisors, that we need to store up more and more treasures for our retirement. Many people who claim to be Christians see no problem or contradiction with what Jesus is clearly stating, because they've been taught that they have met the standard for storing up treasures in heaven by proclaiming their faith in Jesus, so what they do on earth is of marginal importance. Advocating for larger social transformation that would make it unnecessary to hoard as an individual rarely even crosses most Christians' minds.

So, how we can see and understand Jesus' teaching? The spiritual practice of letting go is the antidote to the ego-clinging that creates systems of injustice and oppression.

Embracing Powerlessness and Death

The spiritual life is full of paradoxes. This is true in every tradition, and perhaps the greatest paradox of all is that talking about life honestly requires us to confront and embrace death. One instruction in Christian monasteries was to recall, as you were entering prayer, that "death strikes without warning." In multiple traditions, disciples are taught to pray in graveyards. And these teachings are about spiritual practice in the here and now, not the afterlife. How can this be?

As I've discussed, the ego process is primarily about survival and the maintenance of habit: Once we know we are alive, we wish to stay that way. To maintain ourselves, we also want control over our lives. We wish to be masters of the universe or kings of the world. Of course, we are neither of these things, and there is no better image of our ego's delusion than that scene in the *Titanic* when Leonardo DiCaprio's character yells from a ship doomed to sink that he is king of the world.

The human desire to avoid death is ancient, and many kings, explorers, and now our entire society have devoted themselves to finding eternal, material, youth and life. The life extension industry is a multi-billion-dollar endeavor and covers everything from pills and potions to cryogenic freezing of your body or, for a discount, just your head![17] Hardly a day goes by when we do not hear that "sixty is the new forty" or "eighty is the new sixty." Of course, within this social context, money is needed to live longer and longer; thus, the retirement savings industry is also growing by leaps and bounds.

Yet our bodies cannot live forever, and we cannot control even the majority of what happens to us in our lives. We all *know* this, but we push it to the recesses of our consciousness. Sadly, we commonly respond to events that expose our powerlessness by blaming those who are suffering. Parents with children who are addicts must have been bad parents. Those with illness must not have taken care of themselves. There really aren't accidents; someone must have done something wrong. We think and say these horrible things because it bolsters our sense of control and mastery over our fate. The ego thinks, *If I just do everything right, I'll be fine forever.*

Such thinking creates more suffering, and the spiritual life offers us a distinctly different approach, one that is embedded in Jesus' teaching about material hoarding. Rather than avoiding death and powerlessness, we should embrace them. We should recognize that everything becomes moth-eaten and composts. Those of us who celebrate Ash Wednesday say this every year, but I'm not sure we are truly listening.

As was true with the passage on serving two masters, the key to this passage is at the end where Jesus talks about the focus of our heart. Our heart cannot be in two places, just as our service cannot be in two places. If we and our social order love something that is ultimately empty—as the material world is impermanent and always changing—then we and others will suffer. On the other hand, if we love God, then we have the chance of creating a social order that reduces suffering even if it cannot eliminate material death.

This brings us to letting go, the practice associated with these teachings.

The Practice of Letting Go

One of my favorite phrases is "Give up all hope of fruition." This comes from the Buddhist tradition, and "fruition" here refers to enlightenment, the supposed goal of meditation. This is yet another paradoxical teaching. The idea that I would spend hours at my practice and also give up hope that I would ever achieve the aim of that practice makes no sense to the ego. That is exactly why paradox is a helpful tool.

The ego can always bend logical statements to its will and purposes. As we learn from Ignatian spirituality—one of the great Christian contemplative traditions—human beings are capable of infinite delusion. We may believe we are interested in a spiritual goal involving a change in our ego state, but really our ego is just excited about how good it is getting at being spiritual.

Yet as we practice embracing death and powerlessness, we can practice letting go of both our heart's attachment to material things and, if we are a member of the dominant social classes, to the power that prevents social transformation.

There is nothing easy about this. An obvious example is that White liberals put supportive signs on their lawns but vote against any serious policy change that would lift up people of color and reduce their own power. Ultimately, this is a problem of letting go. Those who have accumulated power wish for a better society but don't want to make any sacrifices to enable societal change. They want to keep their power and the material wealth it brings, and so they continue to uphold the oppressive structures.

This is why all spiritual teachings and communities have embraced renunciation as a part of their communal practice. This has come in many forms, including embracing intentional poverty, changing one's name, leaving one's family, and withdrawing from society. Even the act of coming to prayer at set times—dropping whatever you are doing when the bell rings calling the community to prayer—is an act of renunciation that prioritizes God over projects.

The resistance to letting go of our earthly accumulations can be seen everywhere: Parents will not change their ways to allow for better relationships with their children. People claim to care about social justice and uplift but pass zoning laws to exclude low-income housing in their neighborhood. Churches that have "always done things that way" refuse to change to be more welcoming to new neighbors.

As we continue in our life with God, we consciously draw our attention to our own clinging and the grasping that we see in our communities. We also begin to attend to our relationship with death and powerlessness. In quiet time, journaling, or creative practice, we ask ourselves these questions:

> *What is my relationship with death? Am I afraid of it? Do I deny its existence? How can I embrace the reality of my finitude to find God?*
>
> *What is my relationship with power? Am I a control freak? If so, what does this behavior mask? Is it fear? Is it anxiety? What am I clinging to?*
>
> *What is my social location in relation to power, and am I trying to accumulate it or let go? How does letting go feel? Is it terrifying? What does this say about my relationship to God? How can I make friends with letting go? What do I need to feel safe, to feel supported? As I let go of my material self, can I fall in love with eternal treasures? How do all these questions apply to my communities? Are my communities clinging less or clinging more? What spaces can be created for people who are different from me, for leadership that is different from us?*

The Power of Talking about Money

As mentioned above, there is a reason there is always money for war in the American national budget but never enough for social programs to help the American people at the bottom of the social hierarchy. Like our attempts to even the salary structure in our clinic, talking about money in a way that rearranges our social priorities and empowers those who are currently disempowered is profoundly revolutionary.

When the early church was starting to spread to the heart of the Roman Empire, what was most distressing to the imperial authorities was not new theology or styles of worship, it was the fact that citizens were eating with slaves and the wives of wealthy Romans were allowing their villas to be used for worship gatherings comprised of people from different social locations. It was these concrete material actions, this talk of how to use money in different ways, that was of concern. Because, of course, when we put our money where our mouth is, things happen.

In the same way, White pastors in mainline denominations in the United States often fear that "social justice" sermons will reduce attendance and giving. Or perhaps they are in churches that like hearing such sermons but somehow never change or see themselves as part of the problem. Both sets of behaviors manifest the reality that people in power avoid and discourage serious talk about money and our economic systems.

However, Jesus placed these teachings squarely in his discussion of the beloved community here and now. Jesus could not be clearer that spiritual social transformation requires a transformation of our economic relationships. Our actions show that we are not committed to Jesus' vision of a new reality.

We can see this clearly in our churches. We talk about the "upside-down kingdom" teachings of the gospel, and yet our churches adopt a hierarchical salary structure that exactly mimics the corporate salary structure of the empire. Why should those at the top of the church make the most money?

Why do pastors seek bigger, better calls to get bigger, better salaries? Isn't that exactly like the kingdoms of the world? If the church were to enact an upside-down kingdom, then bishops would make the lowest salary of all, while pastors at the calls that no one wants would have the highest salaries. Imagine what this would do to church organizations. Imagine its witness to the outside world. Now just try bringing this idea up at your next ecclesial gathering, and you will understand very quickly that this practice of letting go may sound simple but is hardly easy.

Now that we have created the communal environment that allows us to listen for God, make space for God, and turn our hearts and our wealth toward God, it is time to move out from here to create a world of justice and peace. We are now ready to explore the practices that relate most intentionally to our interaction with the world. This is the focus of our final three chapters.

10

WHAT IS JUSTICE?
The Practice of Discernment

Beware of false prophets, who come to you in sheep's clothing but inwardly are ravenous wolves. You will know them by their fruits. Are grapes gathered from thorns or figs from thistles? In the same way, every good tree bears good fruit, but the bad tree bears bad fruit. A good tree cannot bear bad fruit, nor can a bad tree bear good fruit. Every tree that does not bear good fruit will be cut down and thrown into the fire. Thus you will know them by their fruits.

Not everyone who says to me, "Lord, Lord," will enter the kingdom of heaven, but only the one who does the will of my Father in heaven. On that day many will say to me, "Lord, Lord, did we not prophesy in your name, and cast out demons in your name,

> *and do many mighty works in your name?" Then I will declare to them, "I never knew you; go away from me, you who behave lawlessly."*
>
> —MATTHEW 7:15-23

Drawn Into the World

This final section of the book consists of three chapters that focus our attention on what a "kingdom" of God looks like from a large, social point of view. All the practices in this book influence how society works and runs, just as Jesus' whole message points toward this society of God. However, the teachings in these last chapters address these issues specifically.

This focus on the nature of society points to another paradox in the spiritual life: Withdrawing into ourselves to focus on God sends us out into the world. As I've mentioned before, I have never understood the idea that church life is some sort of refuge from the world, a place of permanent retreat where we feel superior, protected, and special. That certainly isn't how Jesus lived. His relationship to God drew him into the streets and into constant conversation with people of all social locations. In general, there is very little in the Bible about withdrawal from the world, but there is a great deal about how society should be ordered to create a just society. There is no book of the Bible entitled "Hiding Out," but there are endless stories of how God works with kingdoms and society and how the apostles act in the world.

These chapters bring us back to our initial reflections about the focus of Christianity. Imperial Christianity diffuses the threat of Jesus' revolutionary teachings by directing our desires toward an afterlife. It makes church into a temporary refuge for people who have given up on a better world and are waiting for a future reward. But in the Christianity of Jesus, a life with God is devoted to social transformation that will begin to manifest the beloved community here and now.

God's One Annoying Quality

I like to begin teaching about God's will and justice by discussing invisibility. I see it as God's one annoying quality. I've been challenged about this—at least once by a high-ranking ecclesial official—and have been told that we "see" God in other people, nature, and things like that. But this is the height of "church speak," insider language used by people who already agree on a set of theological assertions about God. Meanwhile, it is obvious even to a four-year-old that God is indeed, in the true and literal sense of the word, invisible.

The claim that there is an intelligent deity in the universe that we cannot see creates numerous challenges for those who claim to follow and listen to such a being, and one of the greatest of these is the issue of God's will. On any given day, you can—though I do not recommend it—scan the internet and find thousands of people who claim to speak for God and know what God desires. Many even claim to be able to know what God wants for you. For a small donation, they will happily share this information with you. How do we know if any of these claims, many of which are contradictory, are true?

This is not a new question, and it's clear from this chapter's scripture passage that Jesus understood this problem. In his example, people are claiming to have done great things in God's name, yet the things they did were their own desires projected onto God. Jesus and Paul both discuss this problem using the metaphor of fruits. When we see a tree without leaves or fruit in the winter, we may not know what type of tree it is. But several months later, when it is laden with apples, we know for certain that it's an apple tree.

The spiritual practice to help us understand God's will, and the one that employs this image of fruits, is discernment, and justice is the main fruit of God's work in the world. Discernment is another simple-but-not-easy practice. In fact, I believe it is the most radical and difficult of all spiritual practices because we are trying to understand the workings of this invisible being. Anyone who has the most basic level of self-awareness knows how hard it is to understand someone else's point of view, even when they are right in front of us and can explain themselves. This is the basic problem in any relationship. Many fights, misunderstandings, and misinterpreted actions or intentions arise between friends and spouses simply because we cannot grasp what the other person is thinking and feeling.

The reason it is so hard to understand another is that the world created by our ego process is incredibly solid, and we are attached to that solidity and perspective. We take our view of reality to be the only view of reality that's acceptable or even possible, and we are at a loss to understand how someone else can see things so differently. Yet when it comes to God, we try to see things from the perspective of a being whose location and existence isn't even obvious to us.

The discernment tradition takes this conundrum very seriously and has a long history of helping people seek God's will in the face of God's annoying invisibility.

Discerning Fruits

The practice of discernment consists of two basic principles and activities. The first is that we must look backward in time to see the fruits of the Spirit to see God's work in our lives. As has been noted, humans are capable of infinite delusion. Thus, we can think that something is "of God," but we may simply be confused and convinced that our ego projects—our preferences and the habitual activities we cultivate—are God's work. However, over time, the true nature of an action becomes clear. The first time an alcoholic takes a drink, it seems wonderful. Years later when their life is destroyed, it is clear that for them drinking isn't so great.

The second important principle of discernment work is cultivating *spiritual indifference*. In the years that I've been doing and teaching discernment work, I've found that this is the hardest aspect of practicing discernment and the hardest principle to understand. Many people assume that it means not caring about things. It sounds cold or callous, but this misunderstanding is just a trick of our ego.

Spiritual indifference is quite like what is now being described as "confirmation bias," which is simply the practice of looking for information that supports our already-held conclusions. Our ego habits, which are the results of our ego process (that three-tiered sorting process), are not just about our actions, but they also influence how we perceive reality. We see what we want to see. Every day on the internet, millions are wasting their time trying to present "facts" to someone they disagree with only to be met with solid resistance and a refusal to acknowledge what may be a basic truth that's staring them in the face. I've had many conversations with people who have walked away from such encounters stunned and dumbfounded, not believing what they've just seen and experienced. Yet this confusion is merely the result of us not recognizing the power of our habitual mind.

In one church I served, there were some who were unhappy with how the governing board was acting and—even though the annual report showed $4 million in the endowment account—I regularly had very intelligent people tell me with a straight face, "The board has spent all the money in the endowment."

Cultivating spiritual indifference is the practice of letting go of our preferences so we can see the fruits accurately. I have been in many situations where the fruits of some activity are those listed in Galatians as fruits that are not of God, yet people have insisted that we must continue those activities because we have always done them that way (see Galatians 5:19-21). This is an example of a lack of indifference. Our ego structures have a death grip on our minds, and they warp our perceptions so that doing the work of discernment becomes almost impossible. This is why the prophets rail against kings who have been blinded to injustice by their own love of wealth and power (see, for example, Elijah and Ahab in 1 Kings 21:17-24).

To practice discernment, we combine these two principles as we seek to understand if an action is "of God." Working to set aside our ego preferences, we look backward—and this can be over a day, or a week, or longer—and ask what fruits came from it. This can be something very small or something large; it can be individual or social. We can ask if something produces "love, joy, peace, patience, kindness, generosity, faithfulness, gentleness, and self-control" (Gal. 5:22-23) or if it produces "enmities, strife, jealousy, anger, quarrels, dissensions, factions" (Gal. 5:20).

Another set of terms in the discernment tradition is "life-giving" and "death-dealing." This comes from the creedal assertion that the Holy Spirit is the "giver of life." Life can be literal life, or it can be a metaphor for things that make us free and fully human. Each person and each community needs to understand what is life-giving and death-dealing for them. This takes time and conscious reflection. For an individual, perhaps we identify what is life-giving or death-dealing by looking at our feelings or sensing how we respond to being in different environments. Perhaps you feel most alive when you are thinking about God or planning. Maybe being at meetings saps your energy and makes you feel lifeless. In a community situation, perhaps the community senses life when they treat children well or invite their neighbors to a meal. On the other hand, maybe they recognize death as they learn that there are vast economic disparities because of certain policies or that a local factory disproportionately causes disease in a poor neighborhood.

As we look backward from the perspective of indifference, we see what actions are producing the fruits of the Spirit and which are not. Moving forward, we are called to do more of what is life-giving and less of what is death-dealing. This is the way of justice and social transformation; it is how the practice of discernment helps us to participate in God's work of forming the beloved community.

The Problem of Justice

Why are there stories from Genesis to Revelation of God's distress at the injustice of human society, even as God gives people the teachings and the tools to do justice? The passage for this chapter gives us glimpse into this problem. The people addressing God are good, well-meaning people. They are not evil or atheists or disinterested in the spiritual life. They have called on Jesus' name; they have preached and prophesied, yet something is amiss.

We seriously underestimate the problem of the human ego process. We can, even when we are interested in God, become quite deluded and confused, caught up in our ego projects, our desire for recognition or our need to be right, or just the basic desire to be loved. The people who are addressing God have paid a lot of attention to what they thought was important, but they didn't take the time to reflect in community on what God wants for the world.

Even the way we relate to the issue of justice reflects this confusion. People often say that justice is a hard thing to define, and in this attempt at obfuscation, we can recognize one of the many tricks that our ego process uses to help us avoid change and transformation. "Hard to define" is the individual and collective equivalent of referring something to committee for further study. If we are convinced that something is too hard to figure out, then we give up.

However, biblical justice is quite simple and clear. The gold standard for assessing justice in society is whether the widows and orphans are cared for. In patriarchal social structures, which have dominated the human social landscape, widows and orphans are detached from social support systems and are therefore disposable. They are the ones most likely to die from hunger and neglect. In other words, caring for widows and orphans is shorthand for caring for everyone. It means that everyone is cared for, everyone has enough to eat and a place to live. That is the definition of justice in the kingdom of God.

However, biblical justice has always been lacking in our world. The hierarchical nature of human society dictates that the few have much more than they need and the many do not have enough. This is the injustice God deplores.

In the United States today, wealth inequality generated by the social arrangements of the worldly kingdoms has reached a degree that was unimaginable even in an empire such as Rome or Babylon. The 750+ billionaires in the US have a combined wealth that is so great that they could feed and house everyone in the US who is below the poverty line on just the earnings of their assets. Yet we, as a society, do not lift a finger to change this arrangement.

Biblical justice is a hard topic not because it is hard to understand but because it strikes at the very heart of the social arrangements of the world. Therefore, it is much easier to ignore, even as we go about our religious activities. Biblical justice requires that those of us who have more than our share give something up, and not just in a charitable sense but in the sense of the structures of society that prop up our ability to have more than others. This is something that our individual and collective egos resist at all costs, but it is what our spiritual life moves us toward.

Practicing Justice and Discernment

As we can see from Jesus' teachings, God is interested in the fruits of justice, not our ideas about positive religious practice. Furthermore, because justice is a social concept—it is society that feeds and houses everyone—our practice of discernment must lead to justice in our communities. So how do we engage this aspect of our spiritual lives?

We begin by practicing discernment in our individual and communal settings. Just doing this work is rare. As I mentioned, cultivating spiritual indifference is very challenging, and we cannot take on large topics related to complex social transformations if we have no personal experience with discernment. Discernment practice is a way of life, not a tool to take out when we have a problem. Just as Jesus came to do the will of the one who sent him, so too we endeavor to do the will of God in every aspect of our being. Discernment is a way of inhabiting the world; we practice setting aside our habitual patterns and ego projects to look for what God is doing so that we might participate alongside the Spirit.

Thus, you might introduce the practice of discernment in your church or your prayer group. Maybe your church council could begin to use discernment practice for doing church business. And you could begin to practice discernment in your individual life as well.

As we start to live with the practice of discernment—especially in groups and communities—we naturally are drawn into the work of justice. The logic is straightforward: If God wants justice and we are doing a spiritual practice that orients us to God's will, then we will be interested in the practice of justice. This is what Jesus means when he says that you will know them by their fruits: A community that practices discernment will naturally bear the fruits of justice.

Every community around the globe has policies that exclude some people from the social contract. These situations and people all need communities that are interested in working alongside them for social transformation. Yet ignorance is one of the most significant obstacles to justice: People with privilege often do not even know of or understand the injustices around them. Discernment work draws us into the world and asks us to learn about the ways the kingdom of God is suppressed. As we draw close to the will of the Divine, we are freed to look at the world as it is and seek its transformation.

I will close this chapter with a very simple example of how this work happens. When I was pastor at a church in a small rural city, there was a homeless shelter in our town where groups could help with the dinner meal. I signed our church up to help, and in my ignorance, I assumed that we would eat with the residents after we cooked the meal. To my surprise, I was told that no other group had ever stayed. In fact, no other group had even cooked at the facility; rather, they all dropped off the meal and left.

Over the years, eating together with families and individuals who were experiencing homelessness changed our church members. They saw what life was like for unhoused people. They got to know one another. Their children frosted cookies together, and it became unmistakably clear that we are all human beings. These meals led directly to social change when members of the church who had power in the city supported funding for programs to help people get housed, get to medical and dental appointments, and transition out of jail more easily. The fruits of justice appeared naturally, even if they were small.

This is how our life with God works: We pray, we attend, we notice, and we work for the coming of the kingdom where there is justice and peace, which is the subject of our next chapter.

11

CREATING PEACE
The Practice of Loving Your Enemy

You have heard that it was said, "An eye for an eye and a tooth for a tooth." But I say to you: Do not resist an evildoer. But if anyone strikes you on the right cheek, turn the other also, and if anyone wants to sue you and take your shirt, give your coat as well, and if anyone forces you to go one mile, go also the second mile. Give to the one who asks of you, and do not refuse anyone who wants to borrow from you.

You have heard that it was said, "You shall love your neighbor and hate your enemy." But I say to you: Love your enemies and pray for those who persecute you, so that you may be children of your Father in heaven, for he makes his sun rise on the evil and on the good and sends rain on the righteous and on the unrighteous. For if you love those who love you, what reward do you have? Do not even the tax collectors do the same? And if you greet only your brothers and sisters, what more are you doing than others? Do not even the gentiles do the same? Be perfect, therefore, as your heavenly Father is perfect.

—Matthew 5:38-48

The Christian Elevator Speech

An "elevator speech" is a marketing term for a succinct explanation of an activity, idea, or product that can be stated in the time it takes to ride with someone in an elevator. I find this whole concept funny because, of course, no one ever talks to one another in an elevator. But writing an elevator speech can be a helpful exercise for clarifying unnecessarily complex ideas. If someone were to ask me what Christianity is all about, I would start my elevator speech with "Christianity is defined by loving your enemy."

The fact that so few Christians have succeeded in following this core teaching should tell us something about the radical and difficult nature of the Christian spiritual life. There are few ideas more endemic to human nature than revenge. Every imperial society and almost every legal code has been built on the idea that one bad turn deserves another. If you do something bad to me, then I need to do something bad to you. This continues today. Violence is a norm of every human society, and revenge is a core concept that continues to drive violent behavior and the threat of violence.

There isn't a single aspect of modern society not defined by an eye-for-an-eye theology. Violent retribution is a cornerstone of our prison system, our nuclear policy, our "welfare" regulations, and our foreign policy. Recently, when discussing the issue of immigration at the southern US border in a retreat setting, I described a story I'd read where border agents were seen pushing children into the river to drown. I commented that if we cannot even agree that drowning children is bad then we are nowhere close to following the teachings of Jesus. Two days later, while reading the news, I saw a self-professed "Christian" defending such behavior by saying, "Well, we have to take care of our own first, and they shouldn't have come here illegally." Plucking out eyes is all the rage.

The kingdom of God is different. Jesus takes on our core beliefs about violence and love and gives us his greatest challenge: *Love your enemy*. Here he is tossing out thousands of years of human habit and behavior and putting peace at the center of this new kingdom. This chapter will examine peace as a spiritual practice and consider how such a practice lies at the center of a life with God and at the heart of spiritual social transformation.

Not about Individual Perfection

Only a religion that has sold out to empire can transform a passage about social behavior, violence, and peace into one about individual morality, and that is exactly what has happened to this part of the Sermon on the Mount. Conventional Christianity has tended to use this teaching as a means of scaring people into believing that Jesus is talking about moral perfection that is necessary for getting into heaven.

There have been entire abusive religious movements, such as the sexual purity movement, based on this idea of perfection as it relates to personal behavior.[18] It is an impressive theological sleight of hand that manages to ignore the entire passage and focus simply on this idea of individual activity as a means of distraction from the violence of empire. Because, of course, if people start thinking about the social ramifications of this passage, then they might begin to question things like a trillion-dollar war budget, or a militarized police force, or even their own behavior toward those with whom they disagree.

We have seen this scriptural malformation with our other passages: Jesus sounds very different if you think he's talking about life after death than if you realize he's talking about life here on earth. Yet again, Jesus is specific and clear that he's talking about earthly existence. He even references the rain and how God is treating everyone on the planet! The concept of an eye for an eye that begins this passage is a relational issue (see Exodus 21:23-27). Jesus is challenging established law codes. Thus, it once again is clear that Jesus is contrasting the kingdoms of the world with the present kingdom of God. Jesus is most certainly *not* talking about individual moral behavior as a ticket to a heavenly afterlife.

What Is an Enemy?

To understand loving your enemy as a spiritual practice, we must begin with the concept of enemy. *What is an enemy?* Because peace is central to every contemplative tradition, the study of enemies has also been a focal point of contemplative teaching: What is it about us as human beings that we always have enemies? Why does this happen? What is the nature and process of our minds that they are always is in the enemy-creation business?

The human ego process with its constant creation of dualities reveals to us the process of enemy creation. The most fundamental and generalized definition of "enemy" is anyone—even including ourselves—who challenges our stable view of reality by contradicting our categories of preferences. We can see this definition at work in Jesus' teachings. He points out that it is normal to love those who love you. People are most comfortable with groups who share their beliefs and perspectives. Then you have "enemies" who have different beliefs and perspectives. The unusual idea is to somehow love those who have a different outlook upon the world.

The Practice of Peace

Our constructed view of the world is complex and multifaceted. It includes everything about our social situation, our place in the world, our religion and understanding about God. When we encounter someone who has a different version and understanding of these things, we immediately feel threatened because our world, which is just *our* world, might fall apart. The Cain and Abel story is an ancient illustration of this problem (see Genesis 4). One brother thinks God likes meat sacrifices; one thinks grains are fine. The question of God's favor and preference becomes threatening, and the result is the first murder. Violence is the common response to the appearance of an enemy: If we can eliminate the threat to our understanding, then we can avoid feeling distressed by the threat to our view of reality.

The practice of peace, encapsulated by the idea of loving our enemies, builds on the idea of spiritual indifference from the previous chapter. We let go of our preferences so that we can listen for God's preference. In the practice of peace, we seek to release our constructed view of the world so that we can listen to another's constructed view of the world. We eschew violence in favor of relationship and compassion.

When we hear the word *peace*, especially in relation to social systems, we tend to think in large terms like war between countries. But peace as a spiritual practice begins with our most intimate and basic relationships. Contemplative communities have always recognized this issue and have placed relational dynamics at the heart of what it means to be in spiritual community. I've mentioned the vow of stability before, and one of the functions of this vow is to aid in the practice of peace. The truth is that we annoy one another a lot! This annoyance is caused by the friction when two egos collide, and this is why the practice of indifference, of letting go of these habits, is essential when we talk about loving our enemies. Our best friend or partner can go from being the person closest to us to our enemy in seconds flat; all they need to do is leave a dirty sock on the floor or a cabinet open in the kitchen.

When we are together with people for any length of time, these annoyances build. Perhaps the first few times we can let them go, but soon we find ourselves thinking about them all the time. We may not notice the stress building in our hearts and bodies, but suddenly we are angry or resentful or even convinced that we can't possibly continue to be with this person. This experience is our ego-self putting up walls between us and the other as it seeks to defend itself against a perceived threat.

Our experience of reality is like what we see in a kaleidoscope: Sometimes we see beautiful coherent patterns, and sometimes we see a jumbled, fractured mess. We move from agreement to war and back again. Our contemplative practice helps us to understand that all the patterns are the same glass, and that they are all temporary, with the light of the Spirit shining through everything. Peace is not the times when we like the glass patterns; peace is seeing the light. In a community where everyone has taken a vow to work through the moments of enmity and practice peace, we can, over time, lessen the power of the ego process and begin to love one another, even though sometimes we are enemies.

Forgiveness and Perfection

The core Christian practice of forgiveness is deeply connected to the practice of loving your enemy. It is what allows us to try again and again to love despite our attachments and habits, but it is also misused and misunderstood. Thus, it is important to recognize what forgiveness is and what it is not.

Forgiveness in not a blank ticket allowing endless abuse. Oppressed people, whether an individual woman in an abusive marriage or an entire group that has been enslaved, have been told to forgive their abusers for centuries. This is another example of imperial religion twisting Christian spiritual teachings to suit its purposes. Because forgiveness is fundamentally a relational practice, it requires both people to participate; it's not a one-way street. This is why I often speak of forgiveness as having both an inner and an outer dimension.

The inner dimension is the spiritual work of letting go of our hurts and our egos' response to being harmed or misunderstood. We engage in the healing that is needed to understand the wrong done to us or to put ourselves in a more empowered position in our lives. This opens us to the potential for outer or relational forgiveness. We are ready to love our enemies, and thus we are at peace in our hearts and minds. The passage for this chapter is addressing this first step, this inner work of forgiveness. As discussed above, contemplative community is a container in which people have agreed to enter both the inner aspect of forgiveness and also the second, outer dimension.

This outer dimension of forgiveness requires that the one who has done the harm is also engaged in this process of transformation. In a rush to forgiveness, the abusive version of this practice forgets that confession and repentance are required before forgiveness is enacted. This three-step process of confession, repentance, and forgiveness has been the core communal Christian practice for centuries. The people who have done us wrong must demonstrate that they understand what they have done and that they are ready to actively work toward change. In other words, they too are working to allow their ego process to fall away and enter the process of transformation. Once these relational requirements are met, then external forgiveness and the restoration of relationship can begin.

Thus, we see how the practice of forgiveness in community leads to a social transformation that can radiate into the world. When we look at the often-misused term *perfection*, we can see that Jesus doesn't mean a static state of goodness in which we never sin or do anything wrong. He means that we are engaging in the process of peace and social transformation. His comment about perfection is in reference to God who sends the rain on both the good and the evil. It is that God is giving all blessings needed for life to everyone. Being perfect is doing good for everyone.

This is an echo of the covenant with Noah when God promises to never destroy the world again: God makes a promise of peace. This doesn't mean that God stops working for good in the world or that God is satisfied with the kingdoms of the world. Quite the contrary. But it does mean that God is committed to transformation that comes through love and spiritual awakening, rather than violence. This is "perfection," and this commitment to the spiritual life is what the kingdom of God asks of us.

The Most Aspirational Practice

We began this chapter discussing how the phrase "love your enemies" is at the heart of Jesus' teachings and is also one of the most ignored of all Christian practices. When we look at our social landscape, it seems as if working for peace is a fool's errand. Yet all the practices in this book have pointed us toward this practice: creating space for God, committing ourselves to our spiritual life, the practice of compassionate relationship and how we use our money, the whole list. These activities prepare us for practicing peace because a person who is aligned with God and focused on the Divine will is capable of anything in pursuit of the beloved community.

The kingdoms of the world practice classic Orwellian doublespeak, telling us that war is peace. This isn't the gospel message. Peacefulness in one section of creation that is sustained by violence elsewhere isn't peace; it's social control. The peace of social transformation is true peace. It is peace that comes through justice: the great image of everyone, unafraid, under their own fig tree (see Micah 4:4).

Thus, communities that commit to the life Jesus calls us into are communities that commit to peace. They are devoted to learning how to let go of themselves so that they may see and understand the other. They desire to enter the mutual practice of forgiveness and deepen their compassion and understanding for one another.

When members of a community do this, they engage in a life with God and are mediators of social transformation. History is full of small examples of how this works. Contemplative communities across all traditions have been mediators and midwives of peace in their parts of the world for thousands of years. Unfortunately, the kingdoms of the world rarely listen to them and almost never understand them. They are often swept aside by war.

However, this doesn't mean we should not keep trying. Jesus calls us to be peacemakers, so let us recommit ourselves and our communities to this most holy of tasks.

12

SOCIAL TRANSFORMATION AND THE COMING KINGDOM
The Practice of Prayer

And when you pray, you must not be like the hypocrites; for they love to stand and pray in the synagogues and at the street corners, that they may be seen by men. Truly, I say to you, they have received their reward. But when you pray, go into your room and shut the door and pray to your Father who is in secret; and your Father who sees in secret will reward you.

And in praying do not heap up empty phrases as the Gentiles do; for they think that they will be heard for their many words. Do not be like them, for your Father knows what you need before you ask him. Pray then like this:

> *Our Father who art in heaven,*
> *Hallowed be thy name.*

Thy kingdom come,
Thy will be done,
   On earth as it is in heaven.
Give us this day our daily bread;
And forgive us our debts,
   As we also have forgiven our debtors;
And lead us not into temptation,
   But deliver us from evil.

For if you forgive men their trespasses, your heavenly Father also will forgive you; but if you do not forgive men their trespasses, neither will your Father forgive your trespasses.
—Matthew 6:5-15 (RSV)

Life with God as Prayer

As we come to the final chapter, we encounter the passage from the Sermon on the Mount that contains what has become known as The Lord's Prayer or the Our Father. My guess is that this prayer has been said more than other prayer in history, or at least it's in the top three. Given that amount of repetition, you might think that people would know that it is clearly about a life with God on earth: We are praying for what God wants here in the present kingdom. But sometimes repetition brings numbness and cluelessness rather than clarity. If you have ever repeated a word so many times that your brain no longer recognizes it or knows what it means, you understand this phenomenon. When we repeat something mindlessly, we pay no attention to the words or to what we are saying. This is certainly the case for the Lord's Prayer and for the teachings about prayer that Jesus says before and after the prayer itself.

This book has been about the practice of prayer for social transformation, and so perhaps one might think that I would have begun the book with a teaching on prayer. However, I think it is best to *end* the book this way because the Lord's Prayer contains teachings on each of the practices I've examined in the preceding chapters. From this point of view, it is a powerful teaching on social transformation.

Throughout history, contemplative communities have gathered to enter this life with God and, as they have done so, they have changed the world around them. Most of the things we now take for granted as being of positive benefit to society—schools, hospitals, care for children, science—have originated in contemplative communities. In times of social decay and crisis, people have always looked to the contemplative disciplines for guidance and a word from God that can provide instructions and inspiration to reform society. But for this positive social change to happen, communities must understand prayer as practice, as a way of life. This chapter will go through these eleven verses and pair them with each of the practices we've explored, summarizing each and showing how this most common prayer can be understood as a powerful vehicle to help us manifest the beloved community.

"And when you pray, you must not be like the hypocrites; for they love to stand and pray in the synagogues and at

the street corners, that they may be seen by men. Truly, I say to you, they have received their reward."

We've all seen our share of loud pray-ers. In one community I served, there was an ecumenical Thanksgiving service that consisted of every pastor in town getting up front and offering a very long, very loud prayer. Mercifully, people stopped coming to the service, and it was discontinued. When we think about prayer as talking to God, it is common for our egos to get in the way and for the prayer time to be about us. Then, if we pray loud enough, perhaps society will reward us by telling us how holy we are, or maybe people desperate for God's favor will fall for our schemes and send us the money we request in exchange for our intercession with God.

This passage is talking about the practice of self-awareness. We must look at ourselves and ask how we engage our spiritual life and what purpose it serves. Are we practicing contemplation because we secretly—or not so secretly—believe it will bring us status or material rewards? If so, we are not following Jesus and need to rethink our commitments. Rather, we practice with the understanding that our prayer life is for the radical purpose of liberation, which is usually at odds with the social norms of the day. We see clearly that society needs to change, and we know that prayer is a powerful vehicle for transforming us and the world around us.

This is why Jesus labels these public pray-ers as hypocrites. He knows that calling on God means calling on a power that will ultimately overthrow the king, and yet those who are praying are reaping the rewards that come from the court treasury. We cannot have both. To have enough self-awareness to take the different and difficult journey to God's kingdom is transformative.

> *"But when you pray, go into your room and shut the door and pray to your Father who is in secret; and your Father who sees in secret will reward you."*

I can imagine the modern response to this passage: "But if it's secret, I won't get any likes, and my great prayer won't go viral." If a prayer is a performance for other people, then praying in secret makes no sense. But Jesus is pointing us toward the practice of serving God. He is reinforcing the teaching that you cannot serve both God and wealth. To pray in secret is to choose to serve God. God's attention is of utmost importance. We don't need thousands of "likes"; we only need God's.

As discussed in the chapter on service, choosing to serve God is hard. Society and our own internal voices tell us this approach to prayer is fruitless. Yet the history of social transformations produced by contemplation tells a different story. Contemplatives from Father Anthony in the desert, to the unknown author called Pseudo-Dionysius, to Hadewijch of the Beguine movement, to Thomas Merton in the twentieth century—and I could make a much longer list—have all gone into their rooms to pray and have, paradoxically, also changed the society around them.

We must remember that prayer isn't about us; it is about allowing the Spirit of God to flow and work through us. The more we engage our spiritual lives, lives which mostly take place in "secret," the more we and our communities can press for the appearance of God's kingdom. That these people became famous shows us the two sides of the same coin of prayer and social transformation: Because the Spirit is always moving outward, our inward work isn't only for ourselves but is leaven for the world.

Yet this passage has been used in service of the status quo. The term "reward" has of course been treated as a reference to heaven; if you pray correctly, you will get into heaven, even if you are poor or oppressed here on earth. But this isn't what Jesus is talking about. Rather, he is contrasting the rewards of empire with the rewards of the spiritual life. A community, and potentially the whole earth, is rewarded as it enters a new way of being in the world. The rewards are the fruits of the Spirit: love, justice, peace. The reward is a life of freedom.

"And in praying do not heap up empty phrases as the Gentiles do; for they think that they will be heard for their many words."

Here Jesus is reiterating his teachings on oaths and authentic relationships. Just as it is easy to say all sorts of things that we have no intention of doing, it is easy to make a prayer of empty words, droning on and on, saying the same things over and over. God hears the same pleas and petitions, the same promises and commentaries but sees no actions for justice.

This is why prayer in the contemplative tradition is about listening. Our focus isn't on the easy work of saying the right things but on listening to the Spirit that calls us to new life and action. This is hard. In activist circles, there is much discussion about "performative activism." This is the activism of empty words. It is putting on a show and saying all the right things before going home and doing nothing with the hope that no one notices. Oaths were the performative activism of Jesus' day. He discourages this and encourages us to practice authenticity in our lives.

> *"Do not be like them, for your Father knows what you need before you ask him."*

So many of our prayers are requests. Somehow God's providence never seems to be enough. Our world isn't enough, even with its almost magical ability to feed, water, and regenerate life. Spiritual teachings never seem to be enough: So much wisdom is repeated again and again down through the centuries. Human beings are never enough. We need more plastic surgery, more letters after our names, more money, more fame. So, we ask God for more.

In this passage, Jesus is alluding to his teachings on anxiety. I often think it's odd that we ask things of a being we say is all-knowing. Logically this shouldn't be necessary. Thus, unconsciously, our praying isn't so much about God but is driven by our anxieties and our need to do something to relieve our stress. We think that perhaps prayer will help. Unfortunately, such reflexive asking God for help prevents us from engaging deeply with ourselves, others, and the Divine. The practice of deeply trusting in the providence of our reality allows us to settle into who we are and what we are called to be and do.

Prayer is the process of listening to what the Spirit calls us to. Social transformation can flourish in this non-anxious space where we allow God's will to be done.

"Pray then like this: Our Father who art in heaven, hallowed be thy name."

The first line of the Lord's prayer brings us back to willful attention, the first practice of this book. Jesus begins the prayer with a declaration that God's name is holy—an assertion of God's fundamental holiness because how we name things reflects their essence—and that God is the Creator of the universe who has taken the royal seat in heaven. In modern terms, we can say that consciousness is an inherent part of reality: We exist in a mindful universe. Holiness is another term for wholeness, goodness, that which is complete; it is what we desire and strive for.

A life with God that moves toward social transformation that reveals the kingdom of God aligns with this holiness. Jesus begins the prayer the same way that the spiritual life begins, with the intention to focus on God. This intention isn't about religious identification that dictates how to focus on God. No, it is about focusing on the one who is beyond all forms because the wholeness of God lies outside the world each of us creates through our ego process. God exists in what we might call "big reality," while each of us resides in "our own world." The contemplative life and the practice of willful attention continually draws us into an ever-widening view, a bigger and bigger world.

The apophatic, meaning "without images," contemplative tradition encourages us to realize that God is *not* any *thing* that we think God is. This is the tradition of nothingness, of a recognition that anything we believe we understand about God is but a dim shadow of God's actual self. This one-pointed focus on God at the center of our lives draws us into this holy darkness, the heart of the universe, this big reality where we encounter the God who is love. The recognition of love, of wholeness, as the essence of the Divine fills us with joy and encourages us to emerge from that center with a powerful desire for social change as we are captivated by the image of a society grounded in love and holiness. Willful attention helps us connect with the basic desire for goodness that lies at the center of our being.

"Thy kingdom come, thy will be done, on earth as it is in heaven."

I laugh a little to myself every time I say this line because I think about all those millions of people and leaders and theologians talking about how Christianity is about going to heaven. *Have they ever heard the Lord's prayer?* The point of Jesus' teachings is right here, evidently hidden in plain sight. The point is for God's kingdom to come here on earth because it is on earth that there is a problem.

Here we have the clearest statement of the intention and point of the spiritual life: the coming of the reign of God, a reign whose existence is revealed by peace and justice.

Therefore, the practice here is the practice of loving your enemy. There is simply no way to construct a society that manifests God's kingdom when the constant threat of violence hangs over the average person. When at any moment, at the whim of some imperial power far away, you can be killed, or your home destroyed, or you can become a refugee, or be internally displaced; when these conditions exist, a life with God on a massive scale cannot happen.

So not only does Jesus point to the purpose of religion—to create positive social transformation—but he also points toward one of the central practices of the communal life that makes that possible: a time when the lion lies with the lamb and swords are beaten into plowshares and we study war no more.

"Give us this day our daily bread."

As we discussed in the chapter on justice and discernment, justice is a simple idea that we make complicated so we can hide how unjust our society is. Biblical justice is about everyone having health and goodness. Everyone is fed, housed, and has the space to engage a peaceful and meaningful life. Here Jesus sums up the concept of biblical justice and points us toward the practice of discernment. Our daily bread doesn't just fall out of the sky; it comes to us in a society that uses resources and has means of exchange that allow people to have bread. The practice of discernment, using the tools of indifference and observing fruits, helps us to see whether our society aligns with this notion of having basic needs. If it doesn't—and most societies don't—this practice also shows how is it falling short and what are paths to enacting God's will.

The United States is the richest country in the world, and every night people go to bed hungry. It is an unjust country. The prayer for daily bread isn't a prayer for bread to fall out of the sky, rather it's a prayer that this aspect of God's will shall be enacted by us. This phrase leads to a key question for discerning the fruits of our society: *We could feed everyone, so why don't we?* As we discern that such a system of care would clearly be more life-giving than the current death-dealing system, our communities will see the changes necessary to promote a just world.

This is how God's kingdom comes into being.

"And forgive us our debts, as we also have forgiven our debtors."

Here Jesus explicitly names the economic practices related to social transformation. Debt is nothing new. In the ancient world, debt slavery was one of the most common means of imperial growth and control. In our era, most of the world's population is mired in individual or social debt, or both. In the US, there are many such examples of the stranglehold of debt: student loans, excessive credit card debt, and the fairly new phenomenon of credit scores (a mysterious number that companies use to justify charging higher interest rates or extra fees for those who can least afford it). On an international scale, the International Monetary Fund, controlled by the US and Europe, holds a financial sword over the necks of billions of people, and the government of China has recently used its wealth to put much of Africa and South America into debt slavery.

When we change the word "debt" to "trespass" or "sin" in our use of the Lord's prayer, we are bowing to the imperial practice of spiritualizing the prayer and having it become part of the personal salvation version of Christianity. Jesus said "debts" for a reason: He was giving us a powerful series of practices to help manifest God's kingdom on earth. With this line of the prayer, Jesus is giving us the practice of letting go of the treasures that are stored and hoarded by the dominant cultures of the earth.

Imagine if all those debts held by those who are the poorest on earth were forgiven. Imagine the trillions of dollars now going to interest payments that would then be freed up for social development and transformation. All that is required for this is for communities in power to let go: let go of their hoarding, of their greed, of their self-enrichment projects. This is how we embrace a life with God.

"And lead us not into temptation, but deliver us from evil."

We don't believe that God leads us into temptation. And, if we are honest, God doesn't do a good job of preventing evil on earth. These tasks are relegated to communities. If the world did indeed manifest the beloved community, it would deliver us from evil instead of leading us into temptation.

Hence this line of the Lord's prayer brings us back to the practice of presence, the practice of being there in the midst of suffering, of creating containers that lovingly hold those who are struggling. It is the practice of communal presence that helps everyone become more loving and transformed. When we are tempted to move back into our ego-based habits and patterns, communities of practice can hold us accountable. When we are tempted by our anxiety, privilege, and the lures of the kingdoms of this world, our communities of practice can help us refocus on our spiritual life.

We have discussed how our spiritual practice increases our awareness so we can make free choices in the world. We fall into temptation and evil not because God makes us but because of our lack of awareness. The mindless nature of our ego-selves causes us to stumble along, careening one way and another like a drunk meandering down the street. In this state, being led into temptation is easy.

"I don't know how that happened" is a familiar line to anyone who has worked with people whose lives have been torn to bits by destructive behavior. It is the awareness generated by life-giving communal spiritual practice that delivers us from such evil and frees us to be present to others as we birth the kingdom of God.

> *"For if you forgive others their trespasses, your heavenly Father also will forgive you; but if you do not forgive others their trespasses, neither will your Father forgive your trespasses."*

These last two passages together show us the problem we face as we consider leading a life with God and the practice of social transformation. In so doing, they point us to the creation of boundaries and humility, two of the most important practices of the spiritual life.

My guess is that most of you who are reading this book, and most Christians who read these lines, consciously or unconsciously, think about heaven and hell and an image of God who is angry, vengeful, and highly judgmental. My experience in numerous retreat settings and working with individuals and groups have consistently revealed that this image lurks not too far below the surface for those who have been raised in church. Recently, I was discussing this with a person, and I asked, "Was there a lot of judgment in your church upbringing?" "It was everywhere," was the tearful reply.

But, of course, Jesus was never like this and if he is indeed one of the clearest visions we have of the Divine, then part of our spiritual work is to rid ourselves of this image.

Remember that the entire point of the prayer Jesus is teaching is to bring the will of God to earth. Thus, this discussion of forgiveness and the positive or negative results of forgiveness must primarily be dealing with how humans are functioning here on earth. When it says that God will forgive our trespasses, it means that God is working with us here and now to enact forgiveness as we are open to it. The primary focus is not that God will let you into heaven; it means that the kingdom of heaven will become closer to earth. Forgiving groups of people manifest the "heavenly" kingdom of God. On the other hand, violent, vengeful people manifest kingdoms that move far away from God's will.

Fearless humility and boundary creation are two core practices needed for social transformation and the manifestation of the beloved community. Here Jesus names our basic stance toward one another as key to the spiritual life. Do we humbly position ourselves for forgiveness and set a boundary against vengeance and hatred? Or do we take the stance of an imperial kingdom, ready to punish and kill anyone who trespasses against what we consider to be right? These are among the most basic questions of the spiritual life, and, sadly, humans choose the latter far more often than the former.

This ego-centered orientation to the world has brought thousands of years of violence, hatred, and death. On earth, God allows us to reap what we sow. The path of forgiveness always means that we can have another new chance, yet, at the same time, humans can always once again choose violence. A heart that isn't open to forgiveness will struggle to receive forgiveness. By contrast, God also gives us the teachings of the spiritual life. God gives us a way out of this endless cycle of revenge: the way of Jesus, the way of peace, justice, and freedom. But we must humbly choose. We are called into communities that set new boundaries, call people to new practices, and seek to transform societies in new ways. We are called into the life of prayer, the life with God. My eternal prayer is that more of us choose God's way.

Let us pray.

NOTES

1. In modern times, the kingdom of God was called the beloved community by Martin Luther King Jr. It has also been referred to as the kin-dom of God by those who desire to eliminate the royalty reference and avoid a masculine descriptor for God. This book uses all three terms interchangeably.
2. See *Creating a Life with God: The Call of Ancient Prayer Practices* rev. (Nashville: Upper Room Books, 2023) and *Leading a Life with God: The Practice of Spiritual Leadership* (Nashville: Upper Room Books, 2006).
3. See the report "Estimated Cost to Each U.S. Taxpayer of Each of the Wars in Afghanistan, Iraq and Syria" from 2022. It is available from the comptroller of the Defense Department. See https://comptroller.defense.gov/Portals/45/documents/Section1090Reports/Estimated_Cost_to_Each_U.S._Taxpayer_of_Each_of_the_Wars_in_Afghanistan,_Iraq_and_Syria_dated_June_2022.pdf.
4. James C. Cobb, "Why Martin Luther King Had a 75 Percent Disapproval Rating in the Year of His Death."

Zócalo Public Square (April 4, 2018), https://www.zocalo publicsquare.org/2018/04/04/martin-luther-king-75-percent-disapproval-rating-year-death/ideas/essay/.

5. For a good discussion about the fact that many people were not cheering the departure of Rome, see Ian Bradley, *Following the Celtic Way: A New Assessment of Celtic Christianity* (Minneapolis: Augsburg, 2020).
6. See Anna Baluch, "Average PTO In The US & Other PTO Statistics (2024)," *Forbes Advisor,* https://www.forbes.com/advisor/business/pto-statistics/.
7. See "Religious Trauma Syndrome," *Wikipedia,* https://en.wikipedia.org/wiki/Religious_trauma_syndrome.
8. See her letters. Her name was Catherine Benincasa, but she is commonly known as Catherine of Siena. Her letters are available in various editions. Project Gutenberg (www.gutenberg.org) has "Letters of Catherine Benincasa" available as a free download.
9. Perri Klass, "How Parents Can Shape a Child's Future with Small Moments of Joy," *Washington Post* (August 5, 2023), , https://www.washingtonpost.com/wellness/2023/08/05/happy-moment-shape-kids-lives.
10. See the map of excessive drinking by county: https://wgntv.com/news/map-shows-which-counties-are-home-to-the-highest-number-of-excessive-drinkers-in-the-united-states/.
11. I am not going to spend time discussing the issues related to the production of the show and whether more actors on the neuroatypical spectrum should have been used. I am well aware of these issues and certainly support a

more inclusive entertainment industry. My reflections here stand despite these concerns.

12. "Rules for Neurotypicals," *Autisticqualia,* https://www.autisticqualia.com/2021/08/16/rules-for-neurotypicals/. The article is meant to be a joke, but it is nonetheless revealing.

13. See, for example, Sarina Gruver Moore, "Autistic Jesus," *Reformed Journal* (April 10, 2023), https://reformedjournal.com/autistic-jesus/.

14. My editor was shocked by my cluelessness about people's concern about pooping. He couldn't imagine that anyone—man or woman—would not relate to this scene.

15. See "Vacant Homes vs. Homelessness in Cities around the U.S.," *United Way NCA* (March 28, 2023), https://unitedwaynca.org/blog/vacant-homes-vs-homelessness-by-city/.

16. See this FAQ from the U.S. Department of Agriculture, https://www.usda.gov/foodwaste/faqs.

17. See Jacquelyne Germain, "200 Frozen Heads and Bodies Await Revival at This Arizona Cryonics Facility," *Smithsonian Magazine* (October 21, 2022), https://www.smithsonianmag.com/smart-news/200-frozen-heads-and-bodies-await-revival-at-this-arizona-cryonics-facility-180980981/.

18. See Clyde Haberman, "How an Abstinence Pledge in the '90s Shamed a Generation of Evangelicals," *New York Times* (April 6, 2021), https://www.nytimes.com/2021/04/06/us/abstinence-pledge-evangelicals.html.

For those who hunger for deep spiritual experience . . .

The Academy for Spiritual Formation® is an experience of disciplined Christian community emphasizing holistic spirituality—nurturing body, mind, and spirit. The program, a ministry of The Upper Room®, is ecumenical in nature and meant for all those who hunger for a deeper relationship with God, including both lay and clergy persons. Each Academy fosters spiritual rhythms—of study and prayer, silence and liturgy, solitude and relationship, rest and play.

With offerings of both Two-Year and Five-Day models, Academy participants rediscover Christianity's rich spiritual heritage through worship, learning, and fellowship. During the Two-Year Academy, pilgrims gather at a retreat center for five days every three months over the course of two years (a total of 40 days), and the Five-Day Academy is a modified version of the Two-Year experience, inviting pilgrims to gather for five days of spiritual learning and worship. The Academy's commitment to an authentic spirituality promotes balance, inner and outer peace, holy living and justice living—God's shalom.

Faculty trained in the wide breadth of Christian spirituality and practice provide content and guidance at each session of The Academy. Academy faculty presenters come from seminaries, monasteries, spiritual direction ministries, and pastoral ministries or other settings and are from a variety of traditions.

The ACADEMY RECOMMENDS program seeks to highlight content that aligns with the Academy's mission to create tranformative space for people to connect with God, self, others, and creation for the sake of the world.

Learn more by visiting academy.upperroom.org.